The Lions and Elephants of
THE CHOBE
Botswana's Untamed Wilderness

To Helen and Dick

Bruce Aiken

The Lions and Elephants of
THE CHOBE
Botswana's Untamed Wilderness

CONTENTS

First published in the UK in 1990 by
New Holland (Publishers) Ltd
37 Connaught Street, London W2 2AZ

ISBN 1 85368 100 8

Design by Bruce Aiken
Maps by Janice Ashby Design Studio

Phototypeset by Hirt & Carter (Pty) Ltd
Reproduction by Hirt & Carter (Pty) Ltd
Printed and bound in Singapore by Tien Wah Press (Pte) Ltd

FOREWORD

HIS EXCELLENCY DR. QUETT KETUMILE JONI MASIRE, LL.D, P.H., J.P., M.P.

With an estimated game population of around 3 million, the same as the cattle population, we in Botswana have to be proud of our wildlife heritage. We are indeed very proud and not only in a theoretical way but in a practical way as can be seen from the fact that National Parks (of which the Chobe National Park is one) and Game Reserves account for 17% of Botswana. Wildlife conservation thus plays an integral part in our national development through tourism in our National Parks and Game Reserves.

The Chobe National Park, which has so attracted the author, is indeed one of Botswana's finest and richest wildlife areas and is seen by many visitors each year. These visitors come both from within but mainly from outside the country. We are proud to share our magnificent wildlife and other local attractions with the rest of mankind as it is our belief that only through human appreciation can such natural resources continue to be cared for for the benefit of both the present and future generations.

It is with this idea in mind that we in Botswana welcome with pleasure the publication of this book which will convey the magnificence of our wildlife and the beauty of our land to people in other countries, and perhaps inspire them to come and see for themselves. When they do come they can always be assured of a warm welcome.

Q.K.J. MASIRE
PRESIDENT OF THE REPUBLIC OF BOTSWANA

'This book is my tribute to

the animals of the

Chobe National Park ...'

AUTHOR'S NOTE

It is said that mother Africa never entirely severs the cord with her offspring. She was always in my mind in those long periods of absence in my twenties and early thirties when I was savouring the delights of other continents. An idyllic childhood spent playing in her fields only increased the appetite for more, for as she cunningly revealed the wonders of one secret, a further two would arise.

My father, an avid reader, weaned me on endless books on Africa – 'Jock of the Bushveld', 'Memories of a Game Ranger', hunters' tales, tribal histories, wildlife manuals, anything related – and when I was old enough, encouraged my exploits into her heart. But even in those days, the continent's wildly accelerating population explosion had claimed most of the hospitable land. Animals were pushed into the remotest areas, often far from their natural habitat, or shepherded into occasional and well-regulated sanctuaries instated to serve as a reminder of a fast-disappearing heritage. It seemed to me that fate had cruelly delayed my existence until it was too late ever to hope of experiencing the joy of untainted wilderness, or feel the earth tremble under the thunder of ten thousand stampeding buffalo hooves.

It was not until the early seventies that I first heard vague mention of some mythical Okavango Swamps – supposedly an unparalleled wildlife paradise. I had no idea of their location, or exactly what they were. Probably just another exaggeration or fantasy. Some years later, when I actually met someone who had fleetingly been there, his almost sacrosanct reverence and descriptions of the area jolted me into immediate and painful retrospection at the lost time of my neglect, and finally, into action.

My initial search for information soon located their precise position in the north-west of the Republic of Botswana, a huge country more than twice the size of Great Britain. Remarkably, the population numbered barely three-quarters of a million, and most of it was situated in the proximity of the south-eastern border. Apart from this area, only the occasional small town or village dotted the map, leaving huge expanses unpopulated but graced by a surprising number of national parks, the majority of which bore names in Bushman or other local dialects.

A four-wheel-drive vehicle was obviously necessary to negotiate much of the territory, and not then possessing such transport, my initial sortie into Botswana was with a safari company. We travelled for several days through a section of the Kalahari Desert, visited the ornithological spectacle of Lake Ngami, saw multitudes of flamingos at the Makgadikgadi Pans, spent some time in the safari centre of Maun, briefly ventured along the crystal-clear waterways of the Okavango Swamps, revelled in the beauty of Moremi, and were amazed at the variety and prolificacy of animals in the Chobe National Park. Yet on culmination of the trip I was left with an emptiness. The past few weeks had provided me with a glimpse of an Africa I had thought long gone – I wanted more.

This first book is my photographic tribute to the animals of the Chobe National Park, they have provided me with so much pleasure and enlightenment over the past three years; and the script, not a scientific treatise, but an opinionated insight into the lives of the Lions and Elephants with whom I have shared so many exhilarating and fruitful hours.

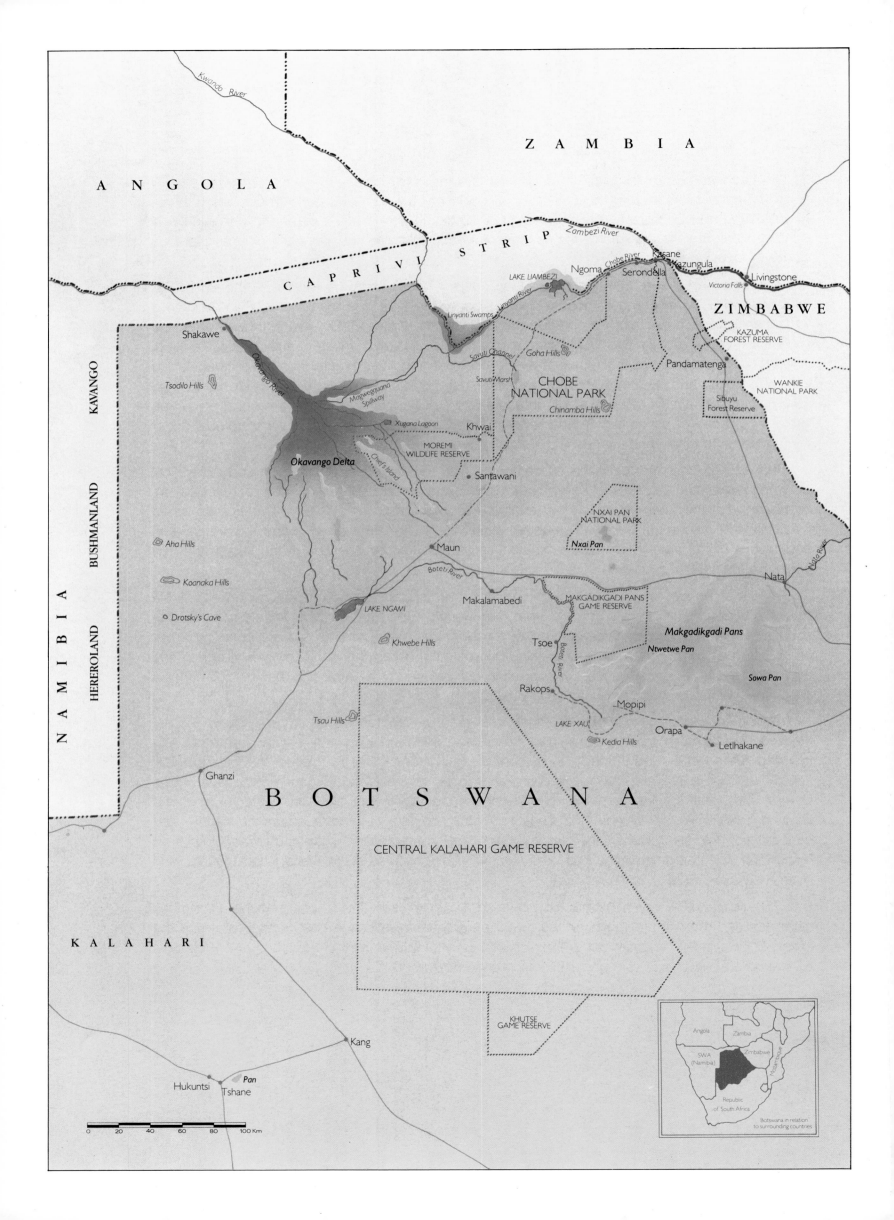

ANGOLA

ZAMBIA

Kwando River

CAPRIVI STRIP

Zambezi River

Chobe River Kasane

Kazungula

Livingstone

LAKE LIAMBEZI Ngoma Serondella

Victoria Falls

ZIMBABWE

Shakawe

Linyanti Swamps

Linyanti River

KAZUMA
FOREST RESERVE

KAVANGO

Tsodilo Hills

Okavango River

Magwegquana
Spillway

Savuti Channel

Goha Hills

CHOBE
NATIONAL PARK

Pandamatenga

WANKIE
NATIONAL PARK

Savuti Marsh

Chinamba Hills

Sibuyu
Forest Reserve

Xugana Lagoon Khwai

Okavango Delta

Chief's Island

MOREMI
WILDLIFE RESERVE

Santawani

NXAI PAN
NATIONAL PARK

Nxai Pan

Aha Hills

Maun

Boteti River

Nata

Nata River

Koanaka Hills

Makalamabedi

MAKGADIKGADI PANS
GAME RESERVE

Makgadikgadi Pans

Drotsky's Cave

LAKE NGAMI

Tsoe

Boteti River

Ntwetwe Pan

Khwebe Hills

Sowa Pan

NAMIBIA

BUSHMANLAND

HEREROLAND

Rakops

Mopipi

Tsau Hills

LAKE XAU

Kedia Hills

Orapa

Letlhakane

Ghanzi

BOTSWANA

CENTRAL KALAHARI GAME RESERVE

KALAHARI

KHUTSE
GAME RESERVE

Kang

Pan

Hukuntsi Tshane

0 20 40 60 80 100 Km

Angola

Zambia

SWA
(Namibia)

Zimbabwe

Mozambique

Republic
of South Africa

Botswana in relation
to surrounding countries

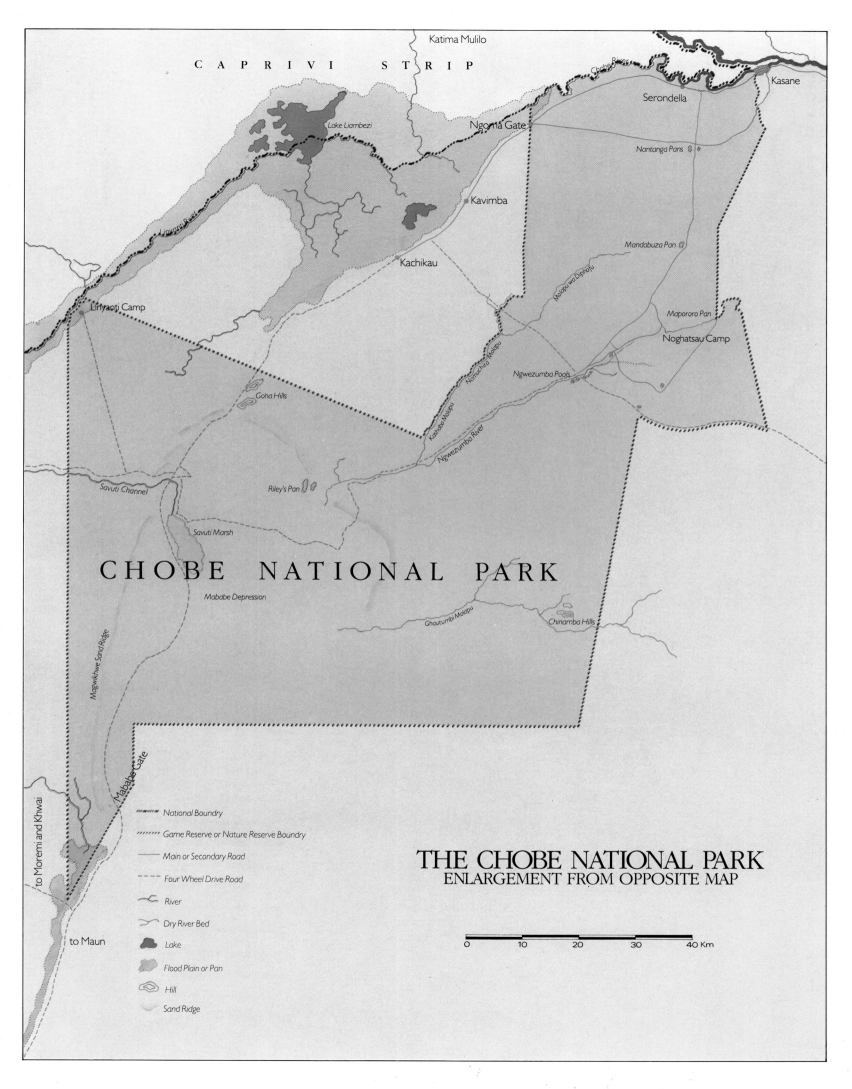

CAPRIVI STRIP

Katima Mulilo

Chobe River

Kasane

Serondella

Lake Liambezi

Ngoma Gate

Nantanga Pans

Kavimba

Mandabuza Pan

Kachikau

Molapo wa Diphofu

Mapororo Pan

Linyanti Camp

Noghatsau Camp

Ngwezumba Pools

Nomachira Molapo

Kashabo Molapo

Goha Hills

Ngwezumba River

Savuti Channel

Riley's Pan

Savuti Marsh

CHOBE NATIONAL PARK

Mababe Depression

Ghautumbi Molapo

Chinamba Hills

Magwikhwe Sand Ridge

Mababe Gate

to Moremi and Khwai

to Maun

National Boundry

Game Reserve or Nature Reserve Boundry

Main or Secondary Road

Four Wheel Drive Road

River

Dry River Bed

Lake

Flood Plain or Pan

Hill

Sand Ridge

THE CHOBE NATIONAL PARK
ENLARGEMENT FROM OPPOSITE MAP

0   10   20   30   40 Km

Page 6 & 7 The Okavango Swamps; almost 15,000 square kilometres of twisting crystal-clear waterways, islands, and oxbow lakes – without doubt one of the world's great wilderness areas.

Page 12 & 13 A herd of Elephants wander through the sparse vegetation in the middle of one of the larger islands. Typical habitat conditions when the floodwaters of May to August fail to reach an area.

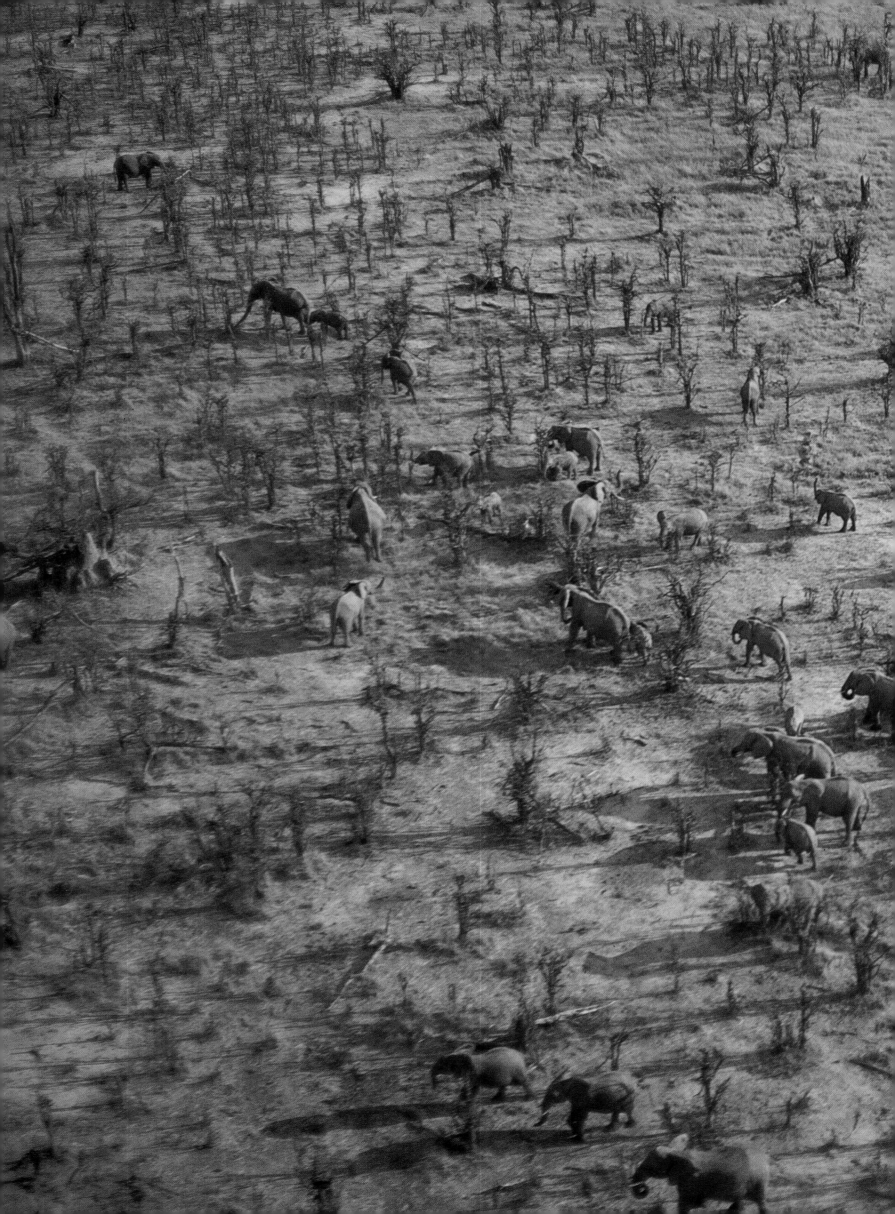

'… I never enjoyed any part of

my wanderings so much …'

Frederick Courteney Selous.

INTRODUCTION
TO `THE CHOBE´

I n the centre of Africa, between the eighteen and twenty-seven degree south latitudes, lies a country containing some of the continent's last remaining great wildlife areas. Here may be found prides of Lions in excess of twenty, Elephants dotting lush plains like so many ants, and huge herds of Zebra, Wildebeest, and Buffalo in their thousands.

Very little of this fascinating country has seen human habitation. Extreme conditions and often virtually impenetrable terrain have left vast expanses largely undisturbed. This is timeless Africa, where today's adventurer can still find new worlds to conquer – not just a reminder of what was; but true Africa in all her remoteness and authenticity.

Seventeen percent of Botswana has been set aside for game reserves. Of these, the Chobe National Park is unquestionably paramount, being host to an incredible number and variety of animals.

Frederick Courteney Selous, one of Africa's most famous explorers and big-game hunters, first visited the area in the eighteen seventies. He wrote: '... I never enjoyed any part of my wanderings so much ...'

Selous was not the first hunter to visit the Chobe, and many followed in his footsteps. In the 1930s, Colonel Rey, struck by the great beauty of the countryside and the immense variety of wildlife, proposed proclaiming the area a game reserve. However, it was not until 1960 that the region was first protected, and 1968 that it was officially declared the Chobe National Park with an area of approximately 11 700 square kilometres.

No fences restrict the movement of animals across park boundaries or bar their access to camping areas. This is Africa virtually untouched by civilisation, where visitors can watch Elephant and Buffalo browsing within yards of their tent, or study a pride of Lions from the safety of a four-wheel-drive vehicle.

Gateway to the park is the colourful village of Maun, approximately one hundred and thirty kilometres south from the Mababe entrance gate. Situated on the banks of a tributary of the Okavango River, one of Africa's largest, it is also the stepping-stone to the fascinating Okavango Swamps; almost 15 000 square kilometres of twisting crystal-clear waterways, islands and oxbow lakes – without doubt one of the world's great wilderness areas.

Maun is the safari centre of Botswana. Immediately one can sense that there is something special about the village. The atmosphere is tinged with excitement as people come and go to the various game-viewing or hunting concession areas. Dust-covered four-wheel-drive vehicles rest outside stores and petrol stations, or busily traverse the village roads. Africans chatter with friends and relatives, making the most of their journey to town to buy supplies.

The village boasts a bank, post office, hotel, airfield, various administration offices, and even a tourist shop. Most of the inhabitants are in some way connected with servicing the surrounding wildlife areas. Safari pilots and professional hunters rest between trips in cool homes along the shady riverbank. Many of the latter, if not most, come from well-known families long associated with the profession.

Fifteen minutes' drive to the north of the village, and situated on a particularly beautiful section of the river, are several establishments offering limited camping or bungalow facilities. Until recently, one such place was the headquarters of a professional crocodile hunter; now, a line of picturesque bungalows graces the riverbank, offering an attractive stopping-off point to the north. A popular meeting place at night, many of the locals and hunters frequent the bar and restaurant, and there is no dearth of interesting conversation – an ideal opportunity to glean information on areas about to be visited. The relaxed atmosphere and appealing surroundings are conducive to staying an extra night or two.

3 Sunrise over the Thamalakane River on the eastern
edge of the Okavango Delta just north of Maun.

INTRODUCTION

A four-wheel-drive vehicle is essential to negotiate the series of small, unmapped, sandy roads which head northwards from Maun. Since surface conditions vary immensely at different times of the year, it is advisable to travel along those roads which have seen the most use. Furthermore, in spite of the short distance, a full day should be allowed for the journey to the park boundary as progress can be slow and it is easy for vehicles to become bogged down in the sand or mud.

As the journey proceeds and the occasional clusters of African huts along the way fall behind, it is evident that one is entering a prolific wildlife area. The sandy roads wind through tall Mopane forests, bright green riverine vegetation, and thick savanna bushland. Beautiful English-type meadows along the Khwai River rival the renowned splendour of the Moremi Game Reserve a few kilometres to the west. Eventually, almost regretfully, one reaches the Mababe Gate, the southern and most popular entrance to the Chobe Park.

Bounded by the Chobe River as its north-east and north-western boundary, the park consists of four main areas: the Savuti Marsh in the west, approximately fifty kilometres north of the Mababe Gate; the lush plains and heavy forestation along the banks of the Chobe River in the extreme north-east, commonly known as Serondella; the hot dry corridor devoid of any permanent surface water, which connects these two areas and, in fact, comprises the bulk of the park; and the beautiful Linyanti Swamps in the north-west.

Most of the park is flat, covered by savanna bush and woodland (predominantly Acacia and to a lesser extent Mopane), interspersed with occasional grassy plains and hilly outcrops. However, in the north-east, particularly along the banks of the Chobe, Mopane, Monongono, Makusi, Mokwa (Bloodwood) and Monato (Rhodesian Ash) dominate.

Very few, if any, of Africa's parks can rival the Chobe's variety and dense concentrations of game. In the north-west, the Linyanti Swamps are home to numerous shy and rarely photographed Sitatunga. Large breeding herds of Elephant and Buffalo congregate at Serondella; whilst the corridor offers a prime example of animal adaptation to harsh conditions. It is at Savuti, however, that the greatest variety of animals can be seen. The large grassy plains surrounding the marsh attract huge herds of ungulates, and consequently a particularly dense predator population.

In this vast wilderness water is the vital determinant of wildlife movement and concentration. Rapidly accumulating clouds interrupt the long hot afternoons of late October, heralding the oncoming rainy season. By mid-November the first heavy rains have usually fallen. Soon, many of the roads become impassable quagmires of mud or slippery clay highways, too tricky even for the most capable four-wheel-drive vehicles.

This is a time of rejuvenation as nature replenishes her larder. Numerous pans throughout the park fill, allowing the huge concentrations of game that have built up around the permanent surface water at Serondella and Savuti to disperse. Often seriously overgrazed and overbrowsed habitat in these areas quickly recovers its former prominence in preparation for the year ahead. Magically, almost overnight, terrain recently denuded of vegetation is covered in succulent rich green grass. There is an over-abundance of food and water for all — except the large predators. For them, the easy pickings of the dry season concentrations are gone. Their hunting prowess will be tested to the full in the months ahead as they follow the widely-scattered game.

For the majority of animals, however, the coming of the rains is a time of great joy. Antelope prance around with new vigour, their coats lustrous and dust-free. Huge herds of Buffalo, Zebra and Wildebeest divide into smaller units and migrate to their favourite pastures. Elephants are free once more to pursue their wanderlust as there is water everywhere. And all rejoice in the young.

Nature in her infinite wisdom has carefully chosen this as the time for most of her progeny to enter the world. Many will perish — especially the weak. But it is the season ensuring most chance of survival. Highly nourishing fresh and short green grass and tender juicy leaves assure a plentiful supply of mother's milk and an easy transition to solids. Predation, although high, is far reduced from what it would be at any other time of year. If the rains are late, many of the animals, especially the antelope, seem to be able to delay parturition. Consequently, a deluge of young populates the Chobe following the first heavy downfall. Nurseries of delicate Impala fawns frolic with childlike delight at their new-found life. Infant Tsessebe, sporting almost impossibly long legs, show surprising turns of speed alongside their fleet-footed elders — the swiftest of all antelope. Litters of comical baby Warthogs, tails high and legs pumping madly, follow single-file behind trotting mothers. Everywhere there is new life. Gone is the tranquillity of the evening meal as endless swarms of insects bombard the campfire light. Attracted by this easy prey, frogs, rodents, scorpions, spiders, and other small predators scuttle about one's feet in a frantic endeavour to secure their fill.

Also accompanying the first heavy rains, are large concentrations of waterbirds which arrive at Savuti to procreate and take advantage of the prolific insect and new vegetable food in and around the quickly-filling pans. And later, as the Chobe covers her floodplains, Serondella presents one of Africa's great ornithological spectacles. Multitudes of pelicans, storks, spoonbills, egrets, herons, geese, duck, teal, jacanas, and crakes, are some of the many species that feed along or on the waterline. Exquisitely coloured Carmine Bee-eaters perform carefree midair acrobatics whilst catching insects to take back to nesting colonies in the riverbank. Brightly coloured kingfishers, rollers, whydahs, European and Little Bee-eaters, are also in profusion. And sovereign above them all are the majestic Fish Eagles. Their eerie and challenging "kow kow kowkowkow's" echo continuously throughout the river-frontage and are to many synonymous with the word "Chobe".

The last of the rains have usually fallen by the end of February. Within weeks the scorching African sun has dried up all the smaller pans and roads. Most of the waterbirds, especially the migrants, have by now left the area. Those remaining, spread out amongst the dwindling food resources. Then, for several months in the afterglow of the wet season, the land is resplendent in brilliant greens — a photographer's paradise. In places, fairytale carpets of waterlilies cover the Chobe River for as far as the eye can see. Emerald meadows provide flattering backgrounds to make even the plainest of animals look beautiful. And then the dry season begins in earnest.

Gradually, one by one, the pans throughout the park dry up. Some of the animals travel straight to Savuti and Serondella; others, simply to the nearest water. The chilly nights and tolerable midday temperatures of short winter months moderate evaporation to some extent, but by the end of August, the heat is back again. September dust devils whirl across the land, and temperatures soar to extremes, desiccating all but a few persistent pans. These become critically overcrowded as animals obstinately cling to their last days in the wilderness — for the corridor is precisely that. Then, on some unspoken signal, the migration from the area accelerates.

This is the time, for a few merciless months until the coming of the rains, that the already well-utilised resources at permanent water points are stretched to the limit. Daily an ever-increasing tide of animals arrives at Serondella and Savuti, drawn to the lifegiving liquid they must have in order to survive. Huge herds of up to five or six thousand Buffalo may be seen sampling the lush grass of the floodplains or that of the marsh. Prides of Lions vie for the choicest territories amongst the plethora of prey; innumerable breeding herds of Elephants gather along the banks of the Chobe River. This is Africa at her most spectacular, a window into the past.

And then the rains fall. The animals rapidly disperse, and nature's cycle continues in her eternal rhythm.

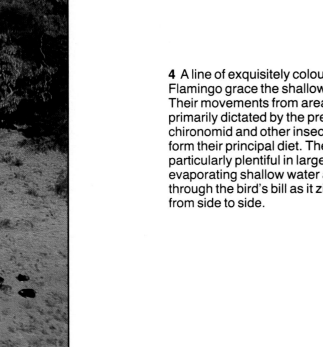

4 A line of exquisitely coloured Greater Flamingo grace the shallows of Lake Ngami. Their movements from area to area are primarily dictated by the prevalence of chironomid and other insect larvae, which form their principal diet. These larvae are particularly plentiful in large expanses of evaporating shallow water and are strained through the bird's bill as it zig-zags its head from side to side.

5 A traditional cattle enclosure near Maun. Natural vegetation (especially Acacia thornbush) is used to make an effective barrier which keeps cattle in and predators out.

SERONDELLA:
THE PLACE OF THE ELEPHANTS

A cool breeze brings some relief from the midday heat as we sit on the hotel's balcony looking out on the Chobe River. A hotel in such a small isolated village as Kasane seems unlikely; equally so, that there are large herds of Elephants only a few kilometres away. At any rate, the view is superb and the cold beer very welcome.

Across the river, more than a hundred metres wide at this point, the open floodplains of the Caprivi Strip stretch to the great Zambisi River, just out of sight below the horizon. A few kilometres to the east, the two rivers converge at the boundaries of Botswana, Namibia (Caprivi Strip), Zambia and Zimbabwe, before flowing over the magnificent Victoria Falls, approximately seventeen hundred metres across and the largest in the world.

Originating in the Angolan Highlands, the Chobe begins its journey as the Kwando, flowing southwards into the Linyanti Swamps. This huge, largely impenetrable sea of papyrus marshland is the home of innumerable Crocodiles, Hippo, Lechwe, and shy Sitatunga, and extends along Botswana's north-eastern boundary, eventually condensing and becoming known as the Chobe River.

Entering Kasane, we notice the headquarters of a well-known safari company. There are also a few stores, an airfield, post office, and the usual police station and district administration offices. As we fill our Land Rover tanks and petrol drums at the village petrol pumps, the unmistakable smell of dead animals pollutes the air. Investigation reveals a depot owned by a large company that purchases skins, tusks, etc. that have been obtained from animals legally shot. Piles of Elephant hides lie stacked one upon another, and Buffalo, Eland, Gemsbok, and Kudu horns are scattered about the ground, no doubt soon to adorn the mantelpieces of elegant homes in the *civilized* world — a solemn reminder that to ensure its continued existence *game must pay*. Temporarily dampened spirits cannot, however, counter the mounting enthusiasm and anticipation we feel on approaching Serondella, legendary breeding ground of Botswana's Elephants.

The awesome size of the African Elephant, up to seven tons in weight and four metres at the shoulder, dwarfs the average motor vehicle. This is the one animal capable of easily penetrating our aloof sanctuary and crushing a car into a heap of tin. No wonder that the inexperienced keep their distance and treat this largest of land mammals with all the respect it deserves.

I can still vividly remember my introduction to Serondella. We had not travelled far from Kasane when an Elephant abruptly stepped out into the road in front of us. We stopped ... just in time, no more than a few paces from the animal. Thick bush had completely obscured its presence until the last moment, and it now turned and faced us, ears outspread and trumpeting loudly, obviously much displeased at our proximity. I hurriedly shoved the Land Rover into reverse intending to make a quick retreat, all the time anxiously keeping an eye on the irate animal who was looking more hostile than ever.

Just then, an ear-splitting trumpet from behind caused me to involuntarily jump several centimetres off the seat. There were Elephants everywhere, leaving no avenue of escape. Somehow we had landed in the middle of a large herd hurriedly making its way to the river. There was nothing to do but sit and hope for the best.

The first Elephant was by now indistinguishable, having merged with the tide of animals crossing the road. We felt very small and vulnerable. Our greatest worry was that one of the numerous animals emerging from the bush directly at the point of the Land Rover would not be able to alter course in time. Virtually every Elephant that passed close by trumpeted loudly and shook a huge head warningly at us and appeared to be about to charge at any moment. It was with a sigh of relief that we saw the last of those Elephants; however, it was some time before the adrenalin stopped pumping.

SERONDELLA

I look back at this incident with great amusement. At the time we were convinced we had had a close shave and were thoroughly shaken. In spite of having spent much time in the bush and game reserves since early childhood, I had not had the opportunity to study Elephants for any length of time. My attitude towards them was one of uncertainty and fear. Today, after several years of close association with these sensitive animals, on foot and from the Land Rover, my feelings have changed to those of deep affection and respect.

Continuing on our journey, we decided to take one of the little sandy tracks down to the open plains and river below. It was late September, almost the height of the dry season, and clouds of dust rose behind us as we descended and came out into the open. I shall never forget that first view of the plains. There were Elephants everywhere, dotted about the lush grass on our side of the river for as far as the eye could see. For some time we sat absolutely still, taking in the spectacle before us, aware that we were witnessing something very special.

Jubilation replaced our initial breathless shock – after all, we had obviously come to the right place to study Elephants. Previously, I had never seen more than thirty or forty at a time. There, on the plains in front of us were literally hundreds. And so, feeling rather elated, we continued on our way.

Situated along one of the most beautiful stretches of the river, Serondella's campsite is an integral part of the park. Simply an area where visitors can pitch their tents. Two small ablution buildings blend inconspicuously into the surroundings, and there are no fences to restrict the entry of animals. The mature attitude of the wildlife authorities in not enclosing such areas provides the visitor with an invaluable opportunity to mix with animals on foot; a good place to learn to walk before one can run.

At the northern end of the campsite, a narrow strip of short green grass some fifteen to twenty metres across and several hundred in length, separates the trees lining the bank from the river. We were sitting here late that first afternoon admiring the view and watching a herd of Elephants a short distance upriver enjoying a mudbath and a swim, when we noticed a large troop of Baboons noisily making their way towards us. They were still some way off, out in the open, and much to my surprise obviously unconcerned about predators. Well over fifty in number, the troop contained many youngsters who were responsible for much of the noise as they playfully chased each other about. On reaching the Elephants, some of them cheekily approached too close, and screeching with delight succeeded in being chased for a short distance. In no time at all we were surrounded – apparently not the only ones to appreciate the view from where we sat. Apart from the odd glance, they paid us little attention, always keeping at least ten metres distant.

There is something special about an African sunset. As the glow of magnificent colours fades, there is the added enchantment as it is not just the end of another day; it is the beginning of a night of excitement and fascination as the bush becomes alive in the age-old struggle for survival. Serondella is renowned for its sunsets, and we were not disappointed on that first night. Engrossed, we watched the red glow on the river fade, then made our way back to the campsite. There we found Baboons everywhere. Adults searched the ground for those last few tasty seeds, roots and insects; youngsters made the most of the final moments of playtime. All were creating an enormous din, and it was only after it had become completely dark that the last of them took to the trees.

That night we listened to an amazing assortment of sounds coming from a few paces away. There were coughs, sneezes, babies screaming, and many other sounds, similar if not identical to those made by humans. Quite a few of the Baboons had settled in the branches of a tree only a few feet above the storage tent, others, slightly further off. In the stillness of night we were able to hear everything as if we had been sitting amongst them, as indeed we were.

We slept little that night. Silence would reign for an hour or so, then a squabble would start, eventually ending in pandemonium with the whole troop vocally participating. In the months to come we would miss them if they were quiet for too long.

Such was my first day and night at Serondella. True there is a large variety of game along the Chobe River; however, there are few parts of Africa, if any, which offer the opportunity of observing several hundred Elephants in an afternoon, or for that matter of sleeping in such close proximity to large troops of Baboons. These two animals, especially Elephants, are the essence of Serondella, and the subjects of the remainder of this chapter.

Early the following morning we made for the same area where we had seen the Elephants the previous day. To our astonishment – no Elephants! For the next two hours we cruised along the edge of the plains spotting only the occasional solitary bull or small bachelor group. By this time the temperature had risen uncomfortably and so, parking in the shade, we awaited developments.

It was not until after midday that distant noises heralded approaching Elephants browsing their way towards the river. The crashing, snapping, and ripping sounds they made as they tore off branches or simply pushed over large trees to get at tasty morsels, sounded much like the advance of a small army. The first herd came down to drink at about two o'clock, but we had to wait until close to four before they began to arrive in large numbers. Soon they were everywhere; drinking, swimming, grazing, having mudbaths, and socializing. In the days that followed, the routine remained more or less the same, although the numbers of Elephants that came down to drink each day varied considerably.

If it were not for their highly sensitive personalities, Elephants could be likened to enormous eating machines. Estimates of the average bull's intake vary immensely, but even in poor habitat conditions a daily minimum of well over a hundred kilograms would be realistic. In order to consume this vast amount, they must spend much of their time feeding, often having to travel many kilometres in search of sufficient browsing and grazing. Their movements, as with most animals, are therefore inevitably governed by the availability of food and water.

Ideally, Elephants prefer to stay as close to water as possible, and this accounts for the semi-devastated vegetation often found in the vicinity of pans and rivers. Such is the case at Serondella. As the dry season progresses, more and more Elephants begin to congregate along the Chobe River. Not surprisingly, they first browse the vegetation closest to the river. Once this can no longer sustain further feeding they are forced to travel further and further afield in their search for fresh food. Consequently, by the end of the dry season, the river-frontage sports a wide belt of badly overbrowsed habitat. Fortunately, with the coming of the rains, there is a mass exodus of Elephants to the corridor and this habitat quickly recovers its former prominence in preparation for the dry season ahead.

Nature has many strange ways. Virtually all, if not all, fit logically into her overall plan. Some are obvious, others less so, and many seem to have no point at all or are unreasonably cruel. Death always has at least one positive result – it provides food for the scavengers and predators so that they may continue living. Most animals die violently, and even to those experienced in her ways it often seems nature could have found a gentler plan. There is often the temptation to break the golden rule and interfere, but as knowledge is accumulated there comes the realisation that it is not for us in our blindness to question nature's laws. No doubt there is a reason for the manner of the Elephant's fate – perhaps because it is too large and dangerous even in extreme age and helplessness for predators to tackle — at any rate, I for one, have always felt nature could have been a little kinder in this instance.

Since fate has decreed that the Elephant spend a good portion — if not the greater portion, depending on habitat — of its life eating, it has equipped the animal with twenty-four highly efficient chewing teeth (molars), six on either side of the lower and upper jaws. Inevitably, all of these wear down through consistent and rough use. When molar number one becomes worn it moves forwards and drops out, and is replaced by molar number two which shifts forwards to take its place. Molar number six is therefore the final molar to come into wear. As it wears down, the animal is able to chew less and less food, and eventually starves.

It is interesting to note that age can be fairly accurately determined by a study of the molars, especially if there are some previous guidelines for the area. Most studies indicate that the first tooth is pushed out before the end of year one, the second at about four, whilst the last molar comes into wear before fifty years of age. It is therefore highly improbable that Elephants live much beyond sixty. Stories of grand old centenarians with enormous tusks would seem incorrect, although there are always exceptions. Tusks are in fact incisor teeth, and continue to grow until death. Very large tusks are probably the result of pronounced growth over a certain period of the lifespan, and not just the result of old age. This becomes immediately apparent when examining any large gathering of bulls at Serondella. Frequently, the largest and therefore oldest bulls have very small tusks, whereas some forty-year-olds already carry outstanding ivory.

Much can be learned by examining an animal's droppings, particularly about its last meal. For instance, those of the larger predators, such as Lion and Hyenas, often contain the hair of the animal they have just eaten and may be whitish in colour — usually the case with Hyenas — due to the calcium content of bones chewed and digested. In instances where other signs are difficult to read, undigested twigs and grass fibres will clearly distinguish between a grazer and a browser, for example between a Black Rhino and a White Rhino. Skilled trackers can often assess an older Elephant's age by examining its droppings. Once the Elephant is on molar number six, its droppings contain more and more undigested food particles as age progresses. Starvation is therefore primarily the result of not being able to chew sufficient food into a digestible form that can be absorbed. As molar number six wears down, the Elephant starts to lose condition. This becomes plainly visible as deterioration advances — the ribs and spine begin to stick out, and the hollows at the temples become more pronounced (Plate 157). Sadly there comes a time when most old ladies and gentlemen can no longer keep up with other Elephants. These old animals, unable to travel great distances, often select an area with plenty of food and water where they peacefully spend their remaining days.

Surprisingly, the mortality rate of Elephants from other than natural causes is relatively high. I often come across one of these huge animals that has succumbed to some illness. Poaching is, however, and will remain, the major threat to the continuation of this species so long as ivory can be legally sold.

The routine at Serondella varied little. Each day would begin and end in the company of our neighbours the Baboons. Not particularly early risers, they descended from their perches in dribs and drabs and made for the strip of grass alongside the river where we had seen them that first evening. There, they plopped down, still half asleep, and enjoyed the warmth of the early morning sunlight for an hour or so before beginning the day's search for food.

I knew of one instance where researchers had, over a lengthy period of time, succeeded in gaining a troop's confidence to the extent of gaining physical contact with the youngsters. It seemed to me that here was an excellent opportunity to attempt to do likewise. Whatever the outcome of my efforts, they would at the least ensure an interesting start to the day and should result in some good photographic opportunities.

It is rude, almost a challenge, to stare directly at an animal. It is also very difficult, if not impossible, to approach most animals by walking straight up to them. My plan was therefore very simple – I would let them approach me.

My first efforts failed dismally. Studiously ignoring them, I would plop down on the bank each morning pretending my sole interest was also to lie in the warm sun. As I lay there, it took a great deal of my willpower not to turn around and see how they were reacting. Fortunately, they always made enough noise to keep me more or less informed of their movements. After several mornings of this it became evident that they were keeping their distance. It occurred to me that they might never come any closer, and deciding to make the most of the situation I rolled over onto my stomach and raised the camera. It could have been gun. Instantly alarmed they ran off, thereafter keeping well out of range.

Disappointed and almost ready to admit defeat I returned to camp. Possibly without a camera their reaction might be different. It certainly seemed worth a try, and the following morning, camera-less, I resumed my place on the bank. Gradually, as the mornings passed, they came closer and closer, eventually finding a limit at about three metres. In time, they became unconcerned about my movements so long as I remained in a neutral position, either sitting or lying down. In fact even if I stood up they would only retreat an extra pace or two. I had obviously been classified as all right and probably eccentric as well, and could now observe them without their becoming nervous.

The male Chacma Baboon, such as found in Botswana, may weigh up to forty kilogrammes and possesses powerful canines which can rip flesh with ease. Their strength is amazing, probably far greater than a man several times their size. Always conscious of their physical attributes, adult males spend much time establishing and displaying their dominance. They do this mainly in two ways: either by forcing the inferior males to give way to them, or by barking. There is considerable status attached to the deepness of a bark, almost like a schoolboy displaying a newly-broken and manly voice. When one of them lets rip, the rest, not to be outdone, usually join in – all trying to go lower than the competition – and collectively making an enormous din. Very annoying for anyone attempting to sleep.

Several large troops usually reside at the campsite, each with their favourite sleeping area. Inevitably their paths do sometimes cross, very often when returning from the day's feeding, and chaos breaks loose. The males then band together into fighting bodies, all the time barking deeply, and gang warfare erupts on a grand scale. For a few hectic moments Baboons seem to be chasing each other in all directions, females continually scream and clasp small babies to their bellies, and dust curtails visibility to only a few feet. Eventually, when all calms down, one expects to see casualties everywhere. Surprisingly, apart from a few minor bites, I have yet to see one of them seriously injured in such a scuffle. Apparently, Serondella's Baboons enjoy a good fracas, but most of it is for show.

Such is the size of the majority of troops that they seem to be completely unconcerned with predation. It is quite usual to see them well out on the open plains, far from cover. Furthermore, when advancing through the bush, they do so with the utmost casualness, seemingly not in any formation (unlike in most parts of Africa). This has always surprised me due to the frequency of predators in the vicinity. No doubt, the unusually large numbers of adult males in most troops are sufficient deterrent to most attackers, as in times of danger they band together to form a formidable protective force.

SERONDELLA

There are no permanent relationships between male and female in Baboon society. During her oestrus cycle, the female's pink callosites (hindparts) swell up to an exaggerated size. At first, during the period of turgescence before maximum fertility, she will normally initiate copulation with a number of less dominant males; even sub-adults who are smaller than she is and must comically and precariously hang on whilst attempting to effect union, their feet too short to reach the ground. When her sexual swelling is most prominent (maximum fertility period), she will usually restrict copulation to the or a dominant male, who will frequently take the initiative himself.

It is almost as interesting to watch people who are watching Baboons, as the Baboons themselves. No other animal elicits such continual reaction from us humans – laughter or sentiment – for in fact we see ourselves in so many of their antics. After all, whether or not one believes in man's evolution from the apes, the physical and mental similarities are both startling and fascinating. Sitting amongst them each morning, I found myself continually comparing and relating human and Baboon behaviour. It seemed possible to me that many of their actions could well provide insight into some of our own. After all, they are living in a society governed only by the laws of nature. Somehow, I have never been able to consider them as just animals, and have always been thankful for their presence on those occasions at Serondella when I have been without human company.

The scene as I observed my troop of Baboons on the bank each morning was in many ways reminiscent of a large group of humans in a similar situation. Adult females, some accompanied by a male, would be scattered about the bank mostly in groups or pairs, keeping a sharp eye on their little pink babies. These play non-stop, chasing each other about, tumbling on the grass, wrestling, and generally getting up to mischief. Slightly older youngsters, when not doing likewise, take much delight in teasing and bullying their smaller brothers and sisters. When things get out of hand, as they continually do, the screaming victim would have to be rescued by admonishing mothers, fast becoming impatient with their offspring. Mature males in their prime sit where they please, very often in the midst of the troop. The older males, no longer dominant, tend to remain on the perimeter. Whereas the younger Baboons, forever playful, would sometimes mimic my actions or simply try and provoke some sort of response out of me, the elder gentlemen were genuinely inquisitive. It certainly was not just a case of my observing the Baboons. Sometimes one of them would stay behind at the campsite for the day. One, in particular, liked to sit and watch me fishing. If there was a moon out, several of these old gentlemen were always visible sitting in trees a few paces away, observing our every move.

There is a curious understanding between the Baboons and the Chobe Bushbuck. These beautiful, chestnut to dark brown coloured antelope, with their clean white vertical stripes, spend most of the day hidden from view beneath thick bushes. Seemingly possessed of little intelligence, they often break from cover, although adequately concealed, at the approach of danger. In the early mornings and late afternoons, it is easy enough to creep up close to them as they browse out in the open since they are not particularly alert. Baboons, on the other hand, are renowned for their capabilities as sentries, and for some reason allow these timid antelope into their midst. The two are completely at ease in each others company, and it is quite common to see younger Baboons touching or holding on to a Bushbuck. Just what the Baboons receive from the relationship I have yet to discover; however, the Bushbuck can relax secure in the knowledge that at the approach of danger the Baboons will sound the alarm.

As interesting as the mornings with the Baboons were, the highlight of the day was definitely the afternoons on the plains. The sense of excitement and expectation experienced when at close quarters with Elephants never abated. Each day would bring some new insight into their behaviour, and this, in turn, often made previous actions meaningful. There is no doubt that the more one learns about an animal, the more fruitful further observations will be.

Every day, after a lazy lunch consumed in the shade of the tall trees lining the riverbank, we would make for a selected section of the plains. As I became more experienced, it was possible to predict with surprising accuracy just when and where we would find the largest concentrations of Elephants. The two most important factors were the previous day's herd movements, and the prevailing weather conditions – especially the wind. It always surprised me how an animal with such an incredibly tough skin could be so influenced by even a slight breeze. Still days meant higher body temperatures and increased thirsts, and invariably saw the largest numbers of Elephants on the plains; while if there was a strong wind, most of them would remain in the bush. Furthermore, the majority usually preferred to graze on the downwind side of an open plain. Whatever rules I tried to formulate there were always exceptions, but fortunately these were comparatively few, and on the majority of afternoons it was possible to successfully select a good observation position prior to their arrival en masse.

An old Elephant proverb states 'No good drinking place is complete without a mudwallow; swimming is very pleasant, but a mudbath is divine'. Elephants are highly gregarious animals, and herd after herd will congregate at the same wallow; firstly drinking at the river, then patiently waiting their turn to roll in the thick juicy mud before assembling closeby for a bit of socialising. Situated at infrequent intervals along the river-frontage, Serondella's well used mudwallows are ideal locations to study Elephant interaction. Although generally sociable animals, they are not partial to noisy vehicle engines and human voices, and seldom tolerate a close approach when out in the open. In time, I discovered that if the Land Rover was carefully positioned prior to their arrival at a spot, close, but in no way interfering with their activities, they would allow much nearer proximity. I feel there were two reasons for this: we were there first, out in the open and making no pretence at hiding our presence; and secondly, they could approach us as closely as they wished, the onus was on them. Elephants are essentially individuals, and as with herds, have had different experiences with humans. On many afternoons we would be surrounded with some only a few metres away, on other days they would retain their distance. Regretfully, it was many months before I accumulated sufficient experience (and nerve) to formulate and effect this method of study. Sitting on the Land Rover roof or quietly on the ground leaning against a wheel, there was always the exhilarating feeling of being 'in the herd', and frequently, interaction with individual Elephants.

It is easy to imagine the thirst these huge animals must feel each day, especially in the extreme temperatures at the height of the dry season, as they complete the long hot journey to the river. Walking eagerly and as fast as possible, a herd will emerge from the bush and make straight for a drinking place, often covering the last fifty or a hundred metres in an abandoned run as they smell the lifegiving water. Unable to restrain their enthusiasm, calves, tails high and squealing with delight, are usually the first to start the stampede and on reaching the river plunge straight in and splash happily away in the shallows. The business of learning to control an unruly trunk needs a lot of practice and very young Elephants, not yet having mastered the art, drink directly from the mouth.

Once immediate thirsts are slaked, adults use their trunks to leisurely spray the cool water all over themselves. Some, especially sub-adults and bulls, are likely to venture out into the river and playfully swim and romp around, often with only the tips of their trunks visible above the surface to act as snorkels. None, however, enjoy themselves as much as the calves. This is the beginning of playtime, and they ceaselessly cavort and chase each other about or even practice drinking with their trunks. In order to perfect this delicate manoeuvre, the water has to be first of all sucked into the trunk. It then has to be kept there (this is the difficult part) whilst the trunk is raised above the level of the mouth and then the water released into it. Always highly demonstrative, they may squeal and shake heads in mock indignation as most of the elusive liquid slops prematurely out of the trunk ending up everywhere but where it should.

Thirsts quenched, it is time for the next and undoubtedly favourite activity, the mudbath. Since Elephants both urinate and defecate in mudwallows and drinking water, the mud is thoroughly contaminated, and this no doubt enhances its effectiveness as a protective coat. Some of the wallows contain a whitish clay which reflects much of the sun's rays keeping the Elephant considerably cooler than would be the case with a darker mudcoat. Visitors can therefore be pardoned for telling tales of white Elephants.

True to form, calves normally dash straight into the quagmire and are soon wriggling about with glee, completely encased in mud. Contrarily, conservative adults slowly and with obvious satisfaction, use their trunks to spray the sticky substance all over themselves. Others, not to be outdone by the calves, assume a variety of comical and contorted positions as they endeavour to cover those special parts of their anatomy, illustrating the remarkable agility of their huge bodies.

Too soon, the old spoilsport cows whose word is law, decide it is time to move off and join the other herds congregating a short distance away. With gleaming wet mudcoats, most of the Elephants pause en route to spray on a finishing coat of the dry reflective whitish sand which is found all along the plains. If conditions were suitable and we had chosen our positions wisely, several herds would, in a short space of time, emerge from the bush, drink, have a mudbath, and gather closeby to graze and socialise.

Herd-size at Serondella varies considerably. Most are between fifteen and sixty – there is no meaningful average. The majority split up, particularly to facilitate easier feeding when numbers become excessive. Typically, a family tree will consist of a primary unit and several sub-units (each of which should be considered as a separate herd and may even be larger than the original unit). If conditions permit, the units will keep in close contact with each other and often join together, particularly for long journeys to a new area. Age and character, rather than physical dimensions, seem to decide which cow(s) will lead a herd. On reaching their early to mid-teens (the age of puberty), bull calves either leave the herd of their own accord or are gradually but forcibly ejected by the mature females who rule the roost. Most of these adolescent bulls join small nomadic bachelor groups. Eventually, when physically mature enough in their mid to late twenties to compete as breeders, they tend to become basically solitary animals, although frequently joining other bulls, and sometimes herds, for periods.

Although bulls generally have an incurable wanderlust, especially very old gentlemen who may often be found in the remotest areas well away from even other Elephants, they do enjoy company and make the most of stays at Serondella. There is one particular spot along the river-frontage, not far from Kasane, which seems to be their favourite gathering place. Apart from containing three mudwallows, it also has a large cut-off lake which makes an ideal swimming location. I have frequently seen in excess of a hundred bulls gathered there, romping in the water, grazing side by side, having mudwallows or just socialising. Younger bulls often enjoy tussles with peers to test their strength, but older bulls past thirty are not prone to this behaviour. All seem to automatically know their place in some tacit hierarchy. On joining a group, smaller bulls sometimes place the tips of their trunks in a dominant bull's mouth, not only as a greeting but also as a gesture of subservience. Another interesting aspect of these gatherings is the frequent mounting of bulls by other bulls (Plate 63). Since the mounter very often has no erection, and a sexual union is physically impossible, this behaviour would seem mainly a method of expressing dominance. One thing is clear, the mounted bulls by their actions leave little doubt that they do not enjoy the performance.

Fundamental to any in-depth study of Elephants is the ability to identify sex and approximate age on sight. Fortunately, during the months spent formulating observation methods, I had become sufficiently familiar with them to do this involuntarily. Sexual identification is complicated by the lack of obvious physical dissimilarities and the fact that the testes are permanently situated in the body cavity. Furthermore, the penis, when not erect is hidden by loose folds of skin. There are, however, subtle differences between the sexes. For example, apart from being much smaller, the female's forehead is narrower and more pointed. At birth both female and male calves weigh about 120 kilograms and have a shoulder height of approximately 85 centimetres. A newly-born male's penis is also clearly visible enabling identification as the folds of skin that conceal it have still to grow. Although for the first ten years of their lifespan there is a minimal height difference, the male is sturdier and increases in weight more rapidly. From the early teens onwards, the difference in both height and weight becomes more and more pronounced until at the end of the lifespan, approximately sixty years, the male stands almost 400 centimetres at the shoulder and weighs up to 6000 kilograms; while the female weighs approximately half of this and has a shoulder height of about 250 centimetres. Both sexes are close to maximum height at thirty, weighing about 4000 and 2000 kilograms respectively, and future growth is mainly confined to increasing their bulk. I have found that an easy method of quick visual comparison between bulls is to compare the distance across the forehead or the top of the trunk between the tusks.

The Elephant's lifespan and social development are in many ways similar to our own. As the afternoons on the plains went by, I began to see young men in their prime, old ladies, aunties, noisy teenagers, and newly-born babies, and not twenty or fifty-year-old male or female Elephants.

Even though the members of a herd are not all related, they do, in fact, function as one big family unit with absentee fathers. All have a highly developed sense of responsibility towards the group, and in times of danger calves are shepherded into a tightly knit kernel with the adult cows forming a protective circle or semi-circle on the outside. One of the saddest sights I have ever witnessed is the common grief displayed by a herd over a dead member. Some of the calves stood with front legs on the body, almost willing it to move, and adults milled around completely disorientated. Undoubtedly a primary objective of their existence as a group is the more efficient procreation of the species, and from birth personalities are shaped towards fulfilling this goal.

Male and female calves begin to show different characteristics by the end of their first year. Whereas males become vigorous play-fighters, indulge in infantile sex play by mounting other calves, and usually develop more individualistic traits, females are generally quieter and less adventurous. Everyone loves a baby, and little Elephants in their first year continually get up to mischief and annoy older brothers and sisters without much fear of retaliation. Mothers, especially those who have not had a baby before, anxiously watch the antics of their newly-born, quickly retrieving them whenever they venture more than a few metres distant. Touch is forever evident, and cows continually fondle calves reassuringly with the tips of their trunks, particularly around the head (Plate 28). Of course there are inattentive mothers, as in any society, but these are very definitely the exception. Cows customarily have several of their calves in attendance, with gaps of at least three years between each, and newest arrivals are normally warmly accepted and looked after by older brothers and sisters. In their first year of life calves are small enough to walk underneath their mothers' bellies, and at first have to stretch to reach a teat. Since they suckle directly from the mouth with the trunk usually folded back over the head, an awkward position, this probably accounts for their habit of drinking often and for short periods. The pinkish teats are similar in appearance to those of humans, and are clearly visible during lactation as they become substantially larger.

From about their second year onwards, calves gain progressively more independence from mothers who no longer keep such vigilant watch over them or intercept so readily whenever playmates become too boisterous. Not yet having acquired a fear of man, two and three-year-olds often advanced on the Land Rover, trunks extended towards us, trying to decide just what this strange object was. An anxious and reprimanding trumpet blast from a nearby cow would halt the approach and, realising that perhaps we were not friendly but not wishing to lose face, they always put on a most impressive threat display before retreating – no doubt enjoying the interlude immensely. I often suspected that the entire performance was put on solely with the end in mind.

Calves rarely lose an opportunity of practising a mock charge, and make a comical sight as they fearlessly advance, ears outspread and trumpeting shrilly, on some unsuspecting Guinea-Fowl or Vervet Monkey. Land Rovers are favourite objects to charge, but only if they are retreating and pose no possible threat. I always remember one particular incident with amusement. Driving along the edge of the plains one afternoon, we stopped for a few minutes to look at a herd. One young bull of about nine or ten was intent on engaging every other calf in a pushing match and was making quite a nuisance of himself. As we moved off, he saw his big chance to impress fellow Elephants and, trumpeting furiously, charged the vehicle with such vigour and determination that he failed to see the thick protruding branch of a dead tree, which he ran into at full tilt temporarily stunning himself. It's my opinion that Elephants have a sense of humour, and I feel sure they appreciated the spectacle as much as we did. It was some time before we recovered our composure sufficiently to proceed on our way. Practising threat displays and mock charges are all part of a calf's training, since on reaching adulthood the victor of most disputes is usually the more audacious bluffer, physical confrontation being extremely rare.

The continual playfighting amongst calves, and later adolescent bulls, also serves a useful purpose in that it brings participants down to size, very necessary with smaller calves, and indicates to them their position on the ladder of Elephant society. Disputes, for instance drinking order priority at a waterhole too small to accommodate all at once, are quickly settled without physical violence as each Elephant already knows its status. These playfights, or more aptly pushing matches, are the opposite of a tug-of-war. The participants face each other, wrap their trunks together or against the opponent's head, and then attempt to push each other backwards. Dramatics add realism and are almost as important as the pushing, and so most contests are accompanied by the fiercest of squeals and trumpeting. Should one of the contestants be larger than the other, he will push just hard enough to win and so ensure a good tussle.

At about two, the milk tusks appear briefly before dropping out and being replaced by permanent ones. Armed with these new weapons, calves soon learn restraint in playfighting since a painful prod is likely to result in angry retaliation from older and stronger brothers and sisters. Youngsters will be youngsters and when opponents become over-zealous, cows usually separate them by placing a trunk between the adversaries.

The average age of first ovulation in females and the equivalent production of spermatozoa in males is about fourteen. For two or three years prior to this, patterns of behaviour in both sexes accelerate appreciably in preparation for the new status to be achieved. Young bulls soon to leave the herd, participate in playfighting with increased vigour and seriousness, consequently spending less time with the smaller calves. At the gatherings on the plains, they would be scattered about in pairs or small groups, continually testing their skill and strength against that of their peers. Sub-adult cows, on the other hand, give vent to strongly rising maternal feelings by playing with or acting as nursemaids to the younger calves. Apart from fulfilling a useful role, this behaviour also serves as good training for when they become mothers themselves. Older, more experienced cows are only too happy to temporarily relinquish the responsibility of looking after their calves to these teenage nannies since this gives them more time to socialise. Mention must also be made of the favourite old aunties and grannies which are continually surrounded by calves. Not every herd has them, but when present, they seem to have a magnetic attraction probably due to highly agreeable and affectionate temperaments, and are seldom accompanied by less than half a dozen adoring youngsters (Plate 61).

Every now and then, a ripple of excitement invades domestic gatherings as two large bulls confront each other. The impact of my first witness to such an event is indelibly imprinted on my memory. Towering above the largest of the cows, with ears outspread to enhance their already enormous appearance, the two Elephants advanced to within a few metres of each other. As the moments passed, the rising tension clearly enveloped all the Elephants in the vicinity. Even small calves curtailed their activities in anticipation, possibly realising the awesome implications of a clash between the two giants. Then, as if on some invisible signal, they closed the gap and placed the tips of their trunks in each others' mouths. Immediately on doing this all tension disappeared.

This procedure is in many ways the equivalent of a human handshake, and although incorrect, I like to refer to it as a trunkshake. It can denote acceptance, affection, or subservience. If, as in the above case, the gesture is simultaneous, then it is used to reduce tension and means mutual acceptance. Should it have been one sided, it would have meant an acknowledgement of subservience by the perpetrator. In more amicable circumstances, adults sometimes show affection for each other in this manner, as do calves towards cows or as a token of respect to large bulls.

The above dramatics occur mainly when there is a possible clash between bulls, usually over a cow in oestrus. Such confrontations at Serondella are almost always tacitly settled, but inevitably serious fights do develop. At such times Elephants can use their tusks on each other with lethal effect, sometimes penetrating an opponent's skull. I have yet to experience a serious fight or to meet anyone who has. Furthermore, after examining numerous skulls scattered about, I have not found one bearing evidence of tusk penetration. Fleshwounds, however, are not all that uncommon. Possibly the sex-mix is such that there are more than sufficient cows to go round. This would seem logical since, due to their larger ivory, bulls are more regularly shot in areas outside national parks than cows. Be this as it may, I have witnessed copulation on only a handful of occasions, this no doubt being largely due to the infrequency of the oestrus cycle.

Apart from being the largest land mammal, the Elephant has several unique features, particularly concerning reproduction. For instance, the female's vagina is ventrally situated, well forward of the hind legs; consequently when erect, the male's penis is disproportionately long and shaped in an 'S' with the tip curving upwards to facilitate entry. The Elephant also has the longest known gestation period, an average of 22 months. As a result, cows are seldom sexually receptive, and then only briefly, since the oestrus cycle is just two to three weeks. Therefore, if a bull is to fulfil his breeding function, he must seize every opportunity.

The strong sexual drive experienced by bulls is clearly evident in their frequent erections during everyday activities. These are visible, indeed hard to miss, since when erect the penis is about 1.5 metres long and often drags along the ground (Plate 39). On coming across a breeding herd, a bull normally examines each female in turn, hoping to find one in oestrus. The great difference in size is nowhere more apparent than during this procedure. With the bull towering over her, the cow normally stands completely submissive as he smells the condition of her vagina with the tip of his trunk; resistance on her part is only likely to lead to aggression. Once satisfied that she is not in oestrus, he will go on to the next cow, and then the next.

The few copulations I witnessed at Serondella all took place well out on the open plains, quite some distance from the Land Rover. Perhaps this was intentional, more likely just unlucky. In the one instance, my attention was drawn to the scene by the considerable commotion and trumpeting as a bull chased a cow. This unusual behaviour did not last long before she suddenly became submissive, probably due to contact, and allowed him to rear up and straddle her with his forelegs resting on her back. Even from the considerable distance, his wildly jerking penis was clearly visible as it extended through her hindlegs, rearing up and down with the tip beating against her belly in a frantic effort to locate the vagina. Once he had effected entry, his pelvic thrusts were brief and accompanied by deep growls, and in total no more than thirty seconds. Throughout the actual copulation, the cow stood passive and silent, externally showing no signs of enjoyment.

Any discussion on Elephant reproduction inevitably leads to several interesting and highly controversial topics. For instance, does rainfall have an effect on reproduction? Or, can Elephants control reproduction in proportion to the amount of food available?

Many animal species in Africa instinctively breed so that their young are born at the most favourable time of the year, and Serondella's Elephants are no exception with the majority of calves entering the world in the lush conditions of the wet season. However, breeding does continue throughout the year, and some unfortunate calves are even born in the harsh conditions of the dry season. It is also noticeable that in certain years there are more births than in others. This does not just apply to Elephants, but to most species in a region. One plausible theory is that animals breed more prolifically in years of good rainfall due to the increased food supplies. Less credible is that they involuntarily and usually correctly predict future conditions. When considering those animals with longer gestation periods, particularly the 22 months of the Elephant, this becomes unplausible.

Human expansion and destruction across the African veld continue to accelerate unabated, and have, of necessity, led to the establishment of sanctuaries to preserve some of this aspect of our heritage. In the confines of these restricted areas, sometimes animal populations inevitably appear, or become, excessive. Fortunately, the Chobe National Park has vast under-utilised areas waiting to be made viable by the pumping up of underground water, should this become necessary, to relieve and divert the pressures of, for instance, the concentration of Elephants at Serondella. Other sanctuaries are often not so fortunate, and then the awesome decision may have to be made 'to cull or not to cull'. Many believe that Elephants can impose self-regulatory restraints on their breeding should conditions warrant this, and there are several good reasons for supporting this theory.

Firstly, there is no doubt that Elephants are able to categorise their range into: safe from humans, definitely not safe, and somewhere in between. Those same Elephants which roam so freely and contentedly at Serondella, amicably tolerating the relatively close approach of visitors to the park, will flee in a mad pathetic panic at the mere whiff of human scent or the sound of a vehicle in border areas or outside the park. They are, therefore, quite capable of distinguishing boundaries, whether restricted or natural, and of acquiring an intimate knowledge of their range. Secondly, Elephants circulate – providing there is water – throughout their range, no matter how vast, in order to take advantage of prime grazing and browsing when and where they occur. The majority will also leave an area which is becoming overbrowsed, such as Serondella at the height of the dry season, as soon as wet season rains fill waterholes elsewhere. It could therefore be argued that if they are capable of assimilating an intimate knowlege of their territory, and of ascertaining the condition of the vegetation and its ability to sustain feeding, they can in all probability realise when to curtail breeding.

Familiarity with Elephants generally leads to a warm feeling of affection for them. After all, they possess many admirable and endearing qualities in terms of human morality. To name a few: the smooth functioning and structure of their society, the devotion of the individual to the group, the importance of touch and affection, the deep emotion displayed over the dead, and the manner in which they often protectively shield and refuse to leave a wounded member. In addition to this, I believe that they clearly possess a superior intellect to most animals, and this is clearly evidenced in their ability for interrelationship with humans. Such interrelationships – especially when one is unarmed and on foot – provide the quickest and most efficient manner of gaining insight into their personalities and answering several particularly interesting questions. For instance, just how well developed are their powers of thought and deduction, and also the senses of smell, hearing and sight?

Any such interrelationships are governed by a new set of rules. No longer can one walk about regardless of the consequences of ignorance and carelessness. After all, man is extremely frail in comparison to Elephants, Lions, Rhinos and Hippos. Yet, in spite of this, there is little to fear from these animals if they are treated with respect and an understanding of their ways. Everyday, thousands, if not millions, of natives safely walk through Africa's wildlife areas in pursuit of their daily existence. Nevertheless, it would be extremely dangerous for the inexperienced to enter the bush unguarded; just as it would for the Kalahari Bushman to wander unguided through the streets of New York.

A fascinating and at times inhibiting factor in my observations is that I am often in the dark as to how well a particular Elephant can see me. Basically, they have a superb sense of smell, more than adequate hearing, and poor eyesight. So acute is their smell that an undetected approach with the wind behind one is impossible. Assuming one walks soundlessly into the wind, sight then becomes all-important. An added complication arises in that this sense varies tremendously amongst individual Elephants. Some seem virtually blind, hardly able to distinguish objects at twenty metres; others can see fairly well at a hundred metres or more.

Then there is the question of an Elephant's ability to analyse what it sees. A good example of how confusing this can be happened to me one afternoon as I was sitting minding my own business some eighty or so metres from a pool in a sunken riverbed. Shortly after a herd came down to drink, an old cow bolted up the bank and briskly advanced in my direction. My first thoughts were that she could not possibly have seen me and there must be some other reason for the excursion. However, such thoughts were quickly dispelled as she began to charge while still a good forty metres distant. Perhaps she thought I was a Lion. If this was so, then her behaviour was not unusual. I stood up and clapped my hands to identify myself, feeling sure she would realise her mistake. Much to my anxiety she never faltered in her stride until at the last possible moment – just as I was about to jump down the four metre bank – she pulled to a halt. Then, instead of withdrawing, she continued her efforts to drive me off. Neither of us was willing to give way, and quite a performance followed before she eventually made off. Instead of going back to her herd she continued in a downwind direction where she apparently caught my scent for the first time. Visibly jolted she turned, and trumpeting alarmedly, raced back to join the others. Long before she reached them they were in full flight as this was not an area where they were used to friendly man. What did she think I was in those anxious moments when only a few metres separated us? She must have had exceptionally good eyesight for an Elephant to have seen me in the first place. Furthermore, the fact that she went into a panic on catching my scent proved she was familiar with man. It was the sense of smell, not sight, that relayed the important message of identification to her brain. This has been apparent to me on numerous occasions, although it is definitely not the rule.

As with most animals, Elephants frequently have difficulty in distinguishing between live and neuter forms. Even the sharpest-eyed antelope suffer from this malady. In early days, I used to build elaborate camouflaged hides in my efforts to observe animals that were not used to humans or associated vehicles with hunters.

In time, I found that a far simpler and often more effective method was simply to sit in the shade beneath a bush with my form blending into the background. Provided one does not make any quick or jerky movements when in such a position, there is little chance of detection. It certainly is a strange feeling to have an animal only a few metres away look straight at one without registering any presence. Recognition of this aspect of sight clarified many previously inexplicable incidents.

As with humans, Elephants are essentially individuals. Even the personalities of the smallest calves vary considerably. It is therefore impossible to lay down any hard and fast rules regarding Elephant behaviour in any given situation. Fortunately, as with most animals, these huge beasts will, ninety-nine percent of the time, visibly indicate their feelings and intentions on becoming aware of a human. Accurate translation of these feelings is therefore of paramount importance in predicting their probable reactions to one's own movements. Human judgement is inevitably involved in any such interpretation, but with sufficient experience it is likely to be correct. In fact, it is probably far easier to predict an Elephant's actions than those of an unfamiliar human.

On becoming aware of one's approach, Elephants will usually stop whatever they are doing and attempt to identify the intruder. If in a protected area where they are used to humans, it is probably a good policy to facilitate identification. In most instances, an Elephant will then simply resume feeding or doing whatever it was previously. Alternatively, if it considers the proximity too close or is unhappy about one's presence, it will probably then show displeasure in the traditional manner by shaking its head, cracking huge ears, trumpeting and kicking up dust (Plate 79). Provided one then remains a fair distance off, all will normally be well; however, the possibility of a charge, mock or genuine, does exist. This is the time the inexperienced are likely to find themselves in trouble, since to mistake the bona fide for sham may prove fatal. The bluff postures are usually easily recognisable to the practised eye, and generally fit into two catagories. The first is comparable to a human shaking an arm and shouting 'scram' at a trespassing dog. The second, running threateningly towards the intruder with all the appearance of genuine intent, but never actually being prepared to risk bodily contact should it stand its ground. To call an Elephant's bluff consequently requires not only a strong nerve, but also supreme confidence in one's judgement, because in the case of error there will be little chance of avoiding physical contact. On the lighter side, the performance may even develop into an amusing spectacle as the huge animal charges the diminutive intruder in an impressive display of accomplished ferocity, only to halt amidst a cloud of dust at the last possible moment (Plate 101). Its bluff called, the Elephant will then either call it a day or back off a few paces and repeat the procedure. This can carry on indefinitely – I suspect even becoming a game – until one of the participants gives way and withdraws.

The power of audacious bluffing, even between species of vastly different sizes, never ceases to amaze me. Supreme in bulk, Elephants are used to the right of way. Nevertheless, their sovereignty is occasionally challenged, sometimes by the most surprising individuals. A comical and not infrequent sight is to see a tiny Blacksmith or Crowned Plover refusing to give way to an advancing Elephant. With wings outstretched and making an incredibly loud and somewhat irritating noise, the strutting bird usually succeeds in causing the beast to alter course away from its nest built in a shallow scrape on the ground. One entertaining incident occurred whilst I was watching about thirty Elephants enjoying a mudbath in a wallow close to the Chobe River. Not too far offshore a Hippo was swimming back and forth, all the time eyeing the Elephants. He was obviously up to something. Suddenly, with mouth open in a threat posture, he emerged from the river and made straight for the wallow. As expected, the Elephants angrily turned and admonishingly trumpeted at the insolent upstart. Undaunted, the Hippo continued to advance. Eventually after much exhibitionism on both sides, the Elephants ceded the wallow. His fun over and looking extremely pleased with himself, the Hippo then casually sauntered back to the river.

Big as a Hippo is, it is dwarfed by an Elephant. Do these largest and most powerful of land mammals occasionally give way to lesser individuals simply in order to keep the peace? Or, in instances such as above, do they seriously believe that a volatile plover or a belligerent Hippo poses any serious threat? My belief is that when faced with an obstreperous individual who is not aware of his place, Elephants are intelligent enough to realise that diplomacy may be the lesser of two evils. There is no doubt, however, that most of them recognise man as a dangerous, if not fascinating, animal. Fortunately, they are able to classify us, as the following example illustrates, and this makes interaction possible.

Late one afternoon, we were parked close to the thick bush on the edge of a particularly wide section of the floodplains, perhaps two kilometres across on our side of the river. As usual, there were numerous herds of Elephants scattered about. The scene was one of peace and domesticity, when five large-calibre rifle shots shattered the silence. Poachers were at work again on the Namibia side of the river – a regular occurrence! Although showing some signs of uneasiness, Elephants within a few hundred metres of the bush stayed where they were. Those far out on the plains began a panic-stricken dash towards safety. One group, possibly the herd that was shot at, were not much more than dots in the distance at the beginning of their sprint. My heart was sore as I watched their pathetic flight, and I felt ashamed to be part of the human race. How could anyone shoot these sensitive and peaceloving animals perversely in the name of sport or for mere monetary gain? On that day, my admiration of Elephants soared to new heights. Instead of fleeing, each Elephant for itself, the herd remained together. Although clearly terrified, cows kept their young protectively grouped in the middle, and the pace was that of the slowest calf. Soon numerous Elephants gathered about us as they reached the safety of our strip close to the bush. There was much trumpeting and movement, and an air of excitement prevailed as they behaved much like humans do after a panic situation. I felt comparable to a traitor. Here we were, sitting safely in the midst of these huge beasts whose lives man had threatened, possibly taken, only a few moments before. Clearly, they distinguished between us and their attackers. Furthermore, they did not hold us responsible for the actions of our fellowman.

6

6 A favourite section of the Chobe Floodplain several kilometres from Kasane showing the Caprivi Strip (Namibia) bordering the river on the left, and the thick Chobe bush and forestation on the right.

7 The photographer and Elephants on the above section of the floodplains. Generally, Elephants are averse to noisy engines or to being approached in the open. However, if a position is assumed prior to their arrival and care is taken not to disturb their tranquillity, they will normally come remarkably close.

7

39

8

9

8 Hippo frolic in one of the larger pools left on the floodplains after the retreat of the Chobe River from its wet season high.

9 Possessed of infinite patience, this Squacco Heron may remain stock still in this position for many minutes until some unsuspecting frog, small fish, or other insect ventures within range of its lightning fast beak.

10 Occasionally heard splashing about in thick papyrus or reeds but rarely seen or photographed, the extremely shy Sitatunga is a truly aquatic antelope. Long hooves enable it to swim strongly and travel across marshland with ease. When disturbed, the antelope often hides by completely submerging itself in water with only its nose protruding above the surface.

11 Pelicans bask in the glow of the late afternoon sunlight. Although common along the Chobe floodplains as they feed on the rich fish resources, their main breeding colonies are further south at Lake Ngami and in parts of the Okavango Delta.

12 Please hurry up and take our picture so that we can go back to play.

13 A magnificent Fish Eagle, fiercely territorial and undisputed feathered king of the river-frontage, stares down from a favourite perch.

14

15

14 At the height of the dry season, gatherings of hundreds of Elephants may frequently be seen on the floodplains as they come down to the river to drink and socialise.

15 A section through a large herd of buffalo. Herds numbering in the thousands are common at Serondella. Essentially nocturnal feeders in this area, they emerge from the thick bush in the late afternoons to spend the nights grazing on the lush grass of the floodplains.

16 Perfectly in step, two White Rhino trot along the plains. In early days, before the declaration of the Chobe National Park, hunters had virtually exterminated the species in this area. More recently, their numbers have been increased by additions from the Natal Parks Board stocks in South Africa.

17 Several species of bream are liberally scattered throughout the Chobe River and the Okavango Delta and provide a tasty and nourishing form of fresh protein.

17

18 Fishermen from across the river in Namibia ply their trade in the age-old mokoro (a dugout canoe carved from a single hardwood tree). The considerable skill needed to stand up and propel one of these unstable craft by pushing on the riverbed with a long pole requires much practice and is usually acquired during childhood.

19 A solitary Elephant ponders in the tranquillity of a Chobe River sunset.

20

20 The beautiful Chobe Bushbuck enjoys a special relationship with Baboons often extending to touch with their youngsters. Baboons are renowned for their capabilities as sentries, and, once in their presence, Bushbuck can browse in peace secure in the knowledge that the alarm will be sounded at the approach of danger.

21 Elephants consider certain Baobabs very tasty; others, only a few paces away, they will ignore. Over a period of months, sometimes years, they whittle the massive trunk away with their tusks until the tree falls.

21

22

25

23

24

22–25 Once Elephants have succeeded in felling a Baobab, much squabbling accompanies its rapid consumption. Apart from containing valuable food resources such as linoleic acid, it seems probable that the pulp has an intoxicating ingredient. Elephants, after feeding on it, often display unusual and aggressive behaviour.

26 The remains after several days of non-stop feeding.

26

28

27 Animal paths traverse a golden sea of sunlit Mopane.

28 Mothers use their trunks to guide and caress newly born calves, never allowing them to wander more than a few paces off.

29 Previous clashes have often established a hierarchy amongst bachelor bulls and in most disputes one Buffalo will normally immediately give way.

30 The prevalent Redbilled Francolin is usually found in coveys of about three to six. They soon lose their fear of humans, becoming frequent visitors to familiar campsites as they feed on the occasional scrap that has fallen on the ground. Their natural diet is mainly seeds, bulbs, shoots and insects.

31 Gemsbok frequent the drier, more southerly sections of the park. They thrive in harsh conditions, supplementing their natural grass diet with a selection of wild cucumbers, melons, fruits and bulbs from which they obtain most of their liquid requirements.

29

31

32 A cow and her calf ignore the water in the main pool to drink from small side puddles where evaporation has resulted in a concentration of salt and other minerals.

32

33 Colourful algae enliven a stagnant Chobe pool.

34 & 35 Immediately after copulation, it is customary for the female Baboon to 'deflea' the male, and then vice versa. For the most part, the 'fleas' are actually crystals which form on the skin and the procedure is enjoyed immensely.

36 – 38

36 – 38 A sequence of predation. Poachers from the Caprivi killed this Rhino for its valuable horn. Vultures have only succeeded in opening up part of the tough skin, facilitating the largely undisturbed laying of eggs by blowflies. Each female lays batches from 50 to 200 eggs which turn into larvae (maggots) in about twelve days. The larvae eject a copious saliva that moistens and digests the meat. They then suck up the resultant broth, digestion having taken place externally. Once the larvae have started to hatch, the carcass is quickly covered in a seething mass of maggots and consumption of all red meat is extremely rapid.

39 An Elephant cow's vagina is ventrally situated, well forward of the hind legs; consequently, when erect, the bull's penis is disproportionally long and shaped in an 'S' with the tip curving upwards to facilitate entry.

39

40

41

40 A large Elephant bull amuses himself by aiming a blow at an unfortunate Buffalo's rump.

41 Trapped in the remnants of a once large pool, a solid mass of Barbel struggle for survival. If the rains come early, some of them will escape the bills and talons of the numerous Marabou Storks, Fish Eagles and Yellowbilled Kites gathered round the scene.

42 An Elephant calf's belligerence meets with not unexpected retaliation. In any event both participants appeared to enjoy the encounter.

42

43 A second Elephant, whilst chivalrously trying to assist a comrade, became stuck in this mudhole himself. Some time later a third bull suffered the same fate. The authorities, after vainly trying to pull them free, had little choice but to dispatch all three.

44 An axe is an effective tool for the arduous task of separating an Elephant's tusk from its skull. Finer cutting is usually done with a skinning knife so as not to damage the precious ivory.

45 The withdrawal of the nerve leaves a surprisingly large cavity extending well towards the tip of the tusk.

45

46 Much of northern Botswana's rainfall occurs in short sharp localized thundershowers. Consequently, in the drier, more southerly parts of the park, some areas may receive relatively good rains over a rainy season, whilst drought conditions prevail closeby. This results in a natural system of grazing rotation as animals congregate on grasses with a higher water content.

47 A colourful orb-web spider (Argiope sp) waits patiently for prey. Once an unsuspecting flying insect has become entangled in its web, the spider will immobilise it using silk threads which it produces from a group of fingerlike spinnerets at its posterior end.

46

47

48 A favourite drinking and swimming location, this attractive white sand beach also contains a popular mudwallow. White clay reflects a greater portion of the sun's rays than a darker mudcoat, keeping an Elephant considerably cooler.

49

50

49 Primarily nocturnal feeders, Serondella's Buffalo spend the days lying about in the shade of the thick bush on the fringes of the plains, chewing cud, and inquisitively observing any passing activity.

50 His mudbath interrupted by the click of a camera shutter, this Buffalo bull angrily glares at the ill-mannered photographer sitting beneath a bush a few paces away.

51 A squirrel welcomes in the morning with its peculiar ratchet-sounding call which serves as an admirable alarm clock for everyone else.

51

52 – 54 Situated at infrequent intervals along the river frontage, Serondella's well-used mudwallows are ideal locations to observe Elephants. True to form, calves normally dash straight into the mud and are soon wriggling about with glee. More conservative adults use their trunks to spray the sticky substance all over themselves. Some, not to be outdone by the calves, assume a variety of comical and contorted positions as they endeavour to cover those special parts of their anatomy, illustrating the surprising agility of their huge bulk.

52 — 54

56

55 An adult Giraffe stares down from his lofty position. Giraffe possess an enormously powerful kick which is easily capable of killing any African predator. However, despite this and their impressive size, they do occasionally fall prey to Lions. These predators trip them up as they gallop in flight, then several pride members hold the struggling beast down whilst one of them effects strangulation by gripping the throat in vice-like jaws.
56 A Yellowbilled Stork probes the mud and shallows for fish and frogs.
57 Jove's Gardenia (Gardenia Spathulifolia), apart from its attractive flowers, bears fruit which the elephants eat.

57

58

58 Perfect timing. Just before hitting the surface this Fish Eagle checked his swift descent so that only his talons entered the water to grasp the unsuspecting fish swimming a few centimetres below.

59

60

59 Most Elephants are highly affectionate, and as with humans, touching is emotionally very important.

60 Mother's love. Serondella's Baboons are particularly prone to eye problems.

61 Sometimes a herd has a favourite old aunty who is continually surrounded by calves. More often than not, this unusually lovable and tolerant temperament towards calves is probably due to the cow's own infertility.

62

62 Elephants have unbelievably tough mouths and are able to chew and digest large Acacia thorns which would easily puncture a vehicle's tyre. The secreting opening a few centimetres behind the eye is the temporal gland; its function and reasons for secreting are not yet known in the African Elephant.

63 Although this behaviour is not common in Elephants past middle age, from their first year onwards bulls mount other bulls. Since their physical attributes make a sexual union virtually impossible and the mounter more often than not has no erection, this conduct would seem mainly a way of expressing dominance.

63

64

64 Two bulls meeting at a waterhole place the tips of their trunks in each other's mouths in the equivalent of a human handshake. After this, all tension disappears and they drink peacefully side by side. If one-sided, the gesture is used to denote subservience, or by calves as a display of affection and respect towards elders.

65 Elephants are surprisingly susceptible to illness and many die as a consequence. This old bull was fortunate, for after spending several days recuperating at a waterhole the swelling in his hindquarters subsided and he recovered in full.

66 A rare find. A freshly broken-off tusk; perhaps a token of an awesome battle, or possibly just the result of over-exuberant play-fighting.

67 A mating pair of White Rhino enjoy an affectionate nuzzle and a mudbath. In spite of their rugged appearance, they are generally not aggressive and often reasonably gregarious. Essentially creatures of habit, each animal, pair, or group, usually has its own territory which is demarcated by laying and regularly maintaining middens (dungheaps) at intervals along the perimeter.

68 Although a solitary feeder, the aptly-named Openbilled Stork is highly gregarious and can often be seen in large flocks along the riverbank. Its oddly-shaped bill is adapted to crushing the shells of its main food source, snails and freshwater mussels. It also likes to eat small fish and, occasionally, frogs.

69 Knobbilled Ducks are particularly fond of the waterlily seeds and aquatic larvae which abound in the Chobe Floodplain. There is probably some sexual status attached to the size of the male's knob since it is largest in the breeding season.

67

68

69

70 A few kilometres to the east of this popular drinking place, the Chobe River converges with the Zambesi River at the boundaries of Botswana, Namibia (Caprivi Strip), Zambia and Zimbabwe before flowing over the magnificent Victoria Falls, approximately seventeen hundred metres across and the largest in the world.

71

A few kilometres to the east of this popular drinking place, the Chobe River converges with the Zambesi River at the boundaries of Botswana, Namibia (Caprivi Strip), Zambia and Zimbabwe before flowing over the magnificent Victoria Falls, approximately seventeen hundred metres across and the largest in the world.

71 After a long, hot journey to the river, much joy is apparent as Elephants embrace the cool and lifegiving water. None, however, enjoy themselves as much as the calves since this is the beginning of playtime.

72 An old Elephant proverb states 'No good drinking place is complete without a mudwallow; swimming is very pleasant but a mudbath is divine'.

73 For several months in the afterglow of the wet season, in places, fairytale carpets of waterlilies cover the Chobe River for as far as the eye can see.

73

74

74 Vervet Monkeys, whose natural diet is mainly vegetarian (leaves, flowers, fruit, roots, seeds, young shoots and bark) supplemented by insects, small rodents, baby birds and eggs, are highly intelligent and soon learn when it is safe to raid unguarded human food left in campsites.

75 Each year from September to March, exquisitely coloured Carmine Bee-eaters migrate to Serondella to breed. Their nests are dug in colonies along the riverbank, carefully positioned to receive a minimum of the days's sun.

76 For a few summer months each year, the Chobe overflows its banks and presents one of Africa's great ornithological spectacles as a multitude of waterbirds feed along the waterline or in the shallows of the floodplain. Particularly prevalent are the gregarious Spurwinged Geese, the largest of their family.

77 A Waterbuck fawn displays a rust-coloured coat which will soon become grey. Few ungulates are born with the same colour coat they will have at maturity.

75

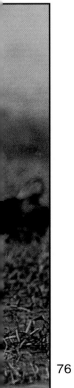

78 An Elephant bull watches the ungainly antics of a companion finding ecstatic relief from an itchy posterior. Although basically solitary animals, bulls are highly sociable and often join other bulls for short periods or even occasionally in semi-permanent relationships.

79

79 An adult cow shakes her head to crack huge ears, trumpets, and kicks up dust in a typical display of feelings aimed at letting us know our presence is not appreciated.

80 Accomplished fliers, Carmine Bee-eaters enjoy performing colourful midair acrobatics to catch insects which they proudly display back at the breeding colony before entering their nests to feed the young.

81 Pathetically refusing to let go of the dehydrated body of her dead child of several days, this mother Baboon resisted all attempts of the troop to take it away.

82 Its valuable horn heavily poached for sale to the East, the once numerous White Rhino has disappeared from most of Africa. Although possessed of adequate smell and hearing, its extremely poor eyesight has led to its downfall, allowing a close and undetected approach from downwind.

87

88

83 & 84 Studies in portraiture: the Vervet Monkey and the Chacma Baboon.

85 The Puku bull, often confused with the Lechwe, has shorter and less divergent horns than the latter. Of the two, the Lechwe is far more aquatic and is often found on small islands. The Puku generally prefers to remain on the open flats bordering a river or marsh.

86 A gallant Lechwe bull. On the approach of danger herds often split up to confuse predators. Firstly, females with young normally go off in the safest direction, then adults in another, whilst the bull will accompany heavily pregnant females at their slower pace until they also reach safety.

87 A pink-faced baby Baboon patiently waits for its mother to finish drinking. When danger threatens, mothers can move at considerable speed with their offspring clinging to their backs or underneath the belly.

88 A young male Chacma Baboon, almost in his prime, exaggerates a yawn to proudly display his impressive canines.

89 Infrequent visitors, flamingos do occasionally visit the Chobe to feed on larvae living in the shallow pools left by the receding floodwaters.

89

90

91

90 A typical confusion of ears as Kudu does stop for a portrait.

91 Motherhood can be a particularly hard time for Vervet Monkeys since, whilst carrying their young, they must also compete with other troop members for food.

92 A Water Monitor momentarily stops digging for eggs underneath a bush. Much can be learnt about the detection of eggs, chicks, and other small mammals by following one of these reptiles as it waddles along in search of food.

93 A baby Baboon – lost in a world of make believe and yellow flowers.

94 Shortly after emerging from its pupa, an as yet unidentifiable butterfly hangs from a twig, its wings crumpled and unformed prior to hardening.

95 The gregarious African Wild Dog, an endangered species, is relatively plentiful in the Chobe National Park. They hunt in packs – often referred to as the wolves of Africa – and rarely stay in one place for more than a few days at a time.

94

95

96 As with humans, the personalities of individual Elephants vary immensely. If bush etiquette is observed, the majority are, however, particularly peaceful and well mannered animals. This group, slowly and in no way threateningly, advances towards the photographer sitting a few paces away on the ground to satisfy their natural curiosity by smelling him.

97

97 Unmistakable because of its brightly-coloured bill, the Saddlebilled Stork usually frequents marshy areas or small pools where it can often be seen tossing its prey (fish, crabs and frogs) into the air, then re-catching and devouring it.

98 An exquisitely patterned butterfly (Cynthia cardui) adds a subtle splash of colour to the river-frontage.

99 A herd of Waterbuck display the comical white toilet-seat markings on their rumps. Bulls are fiercely territorial in defending their areas and harems from competitors. Territories are normally maintained for lengthy periods, sometimes for years on end.

99

98

100

101

100–102 Standing tall with ears outspread to enhance an already enormous bulk, this Elephant charges the photographer. At the last possible moment, its bluff called, the towering animal pulls up amidst a cloud of dust and then retreats a few paces and prepares to charge again.

The performance can continue for some time, almost assuming the proportions of a game, until one of the parties gives way. Unlike the full charge, the mock charge intends no bodily contact and is simply an effort to intimidate and chase off an intruder. It is extremely dangerous for the inexperienced to call an Elephant's bluff in this way, since to mistake the bona fide for sham could well prove fatal.

103 Silhouetted against a delicate African horizon, Elephants joyfully complete the last few steps of their journey to the lifegiving Chobe River.

SAVUTI:
MARSH OF THE PREDATORS

About 180 kilometres north-east of Maun, and centrally situated in the western section of the Chobe Park, lies the Savuti Marsh – possibly Africa's most densely populated predator area.

In 1957, after having been dry for a century, the Savuti Channel flowed once more, entering the Mababe Depression (once a huge lake) through the Magwikwe Sandridge to terminate shortly thereafter in a marshy plain. Attracted to the marsh are a vast number and variety of animals. Africa's big five – Lion, Leopard, Elephant, Rhino, and Buffalo – are all permanent residents. In addition Zebra, Wildebeest, Tsessebe, Waterbuck, Impala, Kudu, Roan, Sable, Eland, Reedbuck, Steenbuck, Giraffe, Crocodile, Hippo, Wild Dog, Cheetah, Hyena, and Jackal number amongst the many local inhabitants.

In spite of this profusion of wildlife, it is the large Lion prides, drawn to the area by the numerous and easy prey, that capture the imagination and interest of most visitors to Savuti. For, as the dry season progresses, more and more Lions follow the steady stream of ungulates migrating to the permanent surface water of the marsh. Consequently, as the concentrations of these animals increase, so do the number of Lion prides, resulting in a remarkably dense predator population: ideal conditions for the observation and study of these largest and most powerful of African carnivores.

The huge herds of Buffalo which gather at the marsh supply the Savuti Lions with much of their food. For many visitors, the Lion/Buffalo interaction is of primary interest. The fact that this is the one regular prey easily capable of inflicting mortal wounds on the king of beasts, no doubt appeals to the romanticism of the human mind. Furthermore, Buffalo, unlike most ungulates, are unable to outrun Lions, and therefore must rely on defence as a means of survival. Sometimes the only viable method of defence is attack, and this adds further spice to these encounters.

The superbly executed and highly logical tactics Lions use in hunting Buffalo and other prey, and their behaviour within the pride, have always fascinated those of us interested in the African bush – my reason for lengthy and absorbing periods spent at Savuti, and the basis of this chapter.

The designated camping area is several kilometres upstream from the marsh, distant enough to preserve the marsh's sanctity, as well as to be relatively free of mosquitoes; and close enough to act as an ideal base. Situated along a section of the channel which is rich in wildlife, the campsite is in itself of interest since it offers valuable opportunities for the exceptionally close interaction with, and observation of, several large and potentially dangerous animals. Elephant bulls, for instance, frequently wander through the area, sometimes singularly, often in the small bachelor groups which are so prevalent at Savuti. Normally very docile fellows, they browse contentedly here and there, taking little notice of campers. They do, however, seem to recognise that this is man's territory, and will normally respect his sovereignty as well as allow a much closer approach than elsewhere. Some of them, more used to people than others, almost lose their fear of man entirely. These old gentlemen will often happily browse within a few metres of humans or gingerly step over a guyrope to reach a tasty morsel in an overhanging tree. So amicable and well-mannered do they appear that there is always the temptation to approach closer than wisdom dictates, or even to feed them. In such a situation it is well to remember that they can be unpredictable and highly dangerous. Sadly, possibly well-meaning but ignorant tourists have at times succumbed and fed them, with unfortunate consequences – so far only to the Elephants. One celebrated bull fondly known as Elroy, once initiated, quickly developed a taste for domestic fruit and began foraging through tents and stationary vehicles. It was only a matter of time before he became a threat to human life, and the park's authorities had little choice but to end his days prematurely.

SAVUTI

There is usually a resident herd of Buffalo at the campsite. All bulls, they spend most days lying beneath the shade of bushes on the opposite side of the narrow channel, quietly chewing cud, and interestedly eyeing the activities of any campers. Essentially peaceful animals unless provoked, they will not normally tolerate a close approach during the day. However, at night, most of their inhibitions vanish as they assume far bolder and often belligerent personalities, and cross over to browse within the campsite. Many a visitor, pants down, and purportedly shielded from prying eyes by the cover of darkness, has had some anxious moments on becoming aware of a quiet chomp chomp a few metres distant. These bulls do, after perhaps a month or more of accustomisation, recognise individual humans. In such circumstances, the bolder amongst them progressively lose much of their daytime caution, eventually becoming regular visitors to familiar camps in the last half hour or so of daylight. Although never quite assuming the effrontery of some of the Elephants, they are generally more at ease in the company of humans, probably inquisitively enjoying the proximity as they feed a short distance off. Most of these bulls have some readily distinguishable physical characteristic enabling quick identification, perhaps the size or shape of the boss, a scar, a bitten-off tail, or a torn ear. This not only facilitates the study of their individual personalities, but also that of the interaction and relationships between themselves – a difficult, if not almost impossible task under normal field conditions.

Another nocturnal denizen of the area is the Hippo. The channel, particularly the section immediately north of the marsh, plays host to a large population of these gregarious herbivores which often weigh well in excess of two tons. My inaugural nocturnal encounter with one of them was to say the least rather dramatic. We had pitched our tent on some short grass close to the channel, and were enjoying the tranquillity of an African night by the campfire, when a gentle splash close by interrupted the silence. Thinking it to be just another fish, we did not feel the noise warranted investigation. However, it persisted, and we looked up into the firelit eyes of a Hippo only a few metres distant. Only his head was above water level, and he glared unceasingly straight at us. Understandably, our imaginations began to work overtime, since there are many fables connected with the Hippo's dislike of campfires. Caution seemed to be a first priority, and so we quickly retreated to within a safe distance of the Land Rover. Then slowly, but without hesitation, the enormous barrel-shaped animal emerged from the channel, and pointedly ignoring us, proceeded to graze a few metres distant. No doubt we had been classified as harmless, or at any rate not hostile. This was the first of many similar, not so anxious, and pleasurable encounters. Since then, I have always made a point of pitching camp along a section of the channel frequented by these enormous herbivores.

The Savuti marsh and surrounding territory can be likened to a large city divided into many residential areas. Some of the inhabitants, for instance Elephants and Wild Dogs, live a transient way of life wandering where they choose. Most of the animals, however, have some degree of permanency to their abode, if only for a few days or weeks at a time. Waterbuck may be found in the same small area week after week. Lions require a far larger territory. Virtually all have a relatively fixed routine as to when and where they are likely to eat, sleep, drink and hunt – therefore, a few months' familiarisation with the marsh enables remarkably accurate prediction as to the whereabouts and activities of any particular animal(s) at a given time, as well as the recognition of permanent residents, newcomers and transients. This is all useful, if not essential information to have when studying predators, since their movements are largely dictated by those of their prey.

All the land within several kilometres of the marsh falls within the territory of some Lion or pride. Since they must regularly kill to eat well, Lions jealously demarcate and then defend their territories (and therefore their sole right to hunt in them) from rivals. Consequently, the choicest territories are generally the domains of the larger and more formidable prides, which are well able to protect their investment. The type of terrain also influences the selection of a territory. For instance, a single Lion will require sufficient cover to stalk or lie in wait for prey; large prides are able to hunt in the open using the age-old tactics to be discussed. Therefore, the flat grassy plains surrounding the marsh, which play host to the largest concentrations of game and offer little cover during the dry season, are divided into the territories of the larger prides. Smaller prides, pairs of males, and the odd single male, establish their territories in the bushy areas on the fringes of the plains or alongside the channel.

A look at Lion family life offers the key to understanding the formation of the different sized prides at Savuti. Typically, a large pride numbers in the twenties. There will usually be two, possibly three, mature males; immature males not yet large enough to be a threat to the dominance of the pride leaders, and the females and cubs which make up the majority.

Mature males should not be considered permanent members of the pride, since in heavily populated Lion areas they are likely to be dethroned by younger and stronger rivals after a year or two. Sometimes they leave the pride of their own accord, possibly looking for greener pastures elsewhere or simply fulfilling a wanderlust. In 1980 one such male was bagged by a trophy hunter outside the park, in an area many kilometres from his old pride's territory. He was a particularly magnificent and aggressive animal, and one of the largest Lions shot in Northern Botswana for many a year. The fact that he and his friend were replaced by far less imposing specimens attests to the authenticity of their leaving for reasons other than usurpation. Although not the rule, mature males are also often less tolerant than females of vehicles, possibly becoming tired of the continual intrusion on the fringes of their dominancy. In my opinion, this was probably the reason for the two grandiose Lions leaving the pride in the above instance.

A Lioness comes into oestrus every few weeks throughout the year. Very often she takes the initiative and presents herself to a male; sometimes she is less predisposed. The pair will normally temporarily leave the pride to mate, copulation occurring approximately every half hour for many hours on end, although the intervals can vary immensely. Since most Lionesses are not prone to absolute subservience, the period immediately prior to each union is usually accompanied by fierce snarling and face-pulling as the male attempts to impress and intimidate his conquest. Once mounted, he may if necessary securely grip the top of her neck in his mouth to ensure co-operation throughout the act. In my opinion, the majority of Lionesses clearly show evidence of deep sensual pleasure during copulation (Plate 170). Gestation is about a hundred days or slightly more, and litter size normally from two to six, tending towards the higher figure. This is probably nature's method of offsetting the high mortality rate experienced by cubs in this densely populated predator area.

A cub's life is a pleasant one. There are normally plenty of brothers and sisters with which to play, and they spend much of their time wrestling or stalking one another — all good training to prepare for actual hunting. Much affection is lavished on them by mother and other pride members, and is apparent between cubs themselves. Adult Lions are noted for their lax habits during the daytime; cubs are forever on the go. Therefore, if there are several litters at once, as is often the case in large prides, cubs will be deposited under bushes or other cover a short distance from the main pride. Here they may play to their hearts' content, exhausting only themselves and the one or two Lionesses whose misfortune it is to act as nursemaids (Plate 159).

In the first few months of their lives, cubs are unable to keep up with adults on night-time hunts. If the pride is large and the prey plentiful, one or even two Lionesses may be left to guard them. In such circumstances, providing there is food to spare, the nursemaids and cubs will be summoned to kills by a series of low belly calls which Lions use to communicate with each other. If the pride is small, all the Lionesses may be needed for the hunt. On such occasions, cubs are left alone for many hours on end. This is a particularly dangerous time for them, even though they instinctively remain hidden and silent. Their hated enemy the Hyena will not hesitate to kill and then eat them should the opportunity occur. Foreign Lions, especially males intent on safeguarding future dominancy, may also do likewise. The mortality rate amongst male cubs is therefore particularly high. Eleven out of the fifteen cubs of one of the larger prides went missing in a single night in 1980, despite the fact that they were probably accompanied by a nursemaid.

Cubs develop incisors at about three weeks, and canines at four. Soon after this they begin to eat meat. Their first attempts to separate a juicy morsel from the main carcass are filled with frustration as their teeth are too small to be efficient. Comically, they assume a variety of undignified contortions in an effort to pull, rather than bite, a piece free. However, by the time they are a few months old they are well able to gluttonise themselves, never seeming to know when to stop eating. Their impossibly full bellies often almost touch the ground, appearing about to burst at any moment. Adult males can consume nearly a quarter of their body weight in one meal, and cubs at least this percentage, a very useful ability if meals are infrequent.

For the first year of their lives, Lions are totally dependent on the guidance and authority of their mothers and other pride members. Their permanent canines appear at about fourteen or fifteen months, and it is only after this that they normally begin to actively participate in killing small prey. Physical maturity is almost complete by the time they are three and a half; however, both sexes do continue growing until about six, although this is confined mainly to filling out and becoming more solid. Lions are said to live up to about thirty years of age, and should a Lioness remain in the pride after attaining adulthood, a perpetual bond of affection usually remains between mother and daughter. In fact much affection and harmony is generally apparent between all pride members (except for some snarling and position jockeying in instances where kills are too small to provide sufficient meat for all). This is not surprising, since for effective survival all are interdependent and must combine and co-ordinate their talents. Nowhere is this more apparent than in the mutual suckling of cubs. This applies not only if a mother's milk dries up, but also under normal everyday conditions. Nevertheless, a Lioness will usually give her own cubs preference if there is competition for a teat.

On reaching two and a half to three years of age, Lions are well trained and capable killers. Since they have not yet attained sufficient physical stature to command a respectable position on the feeding register, they will often receive no share of the spoils at kills – even if their own. For instance, a Buffalo calf or an Impala will provide food for only the pride males and a few of the larger females. Consequently, sub-adult females of this age, possibly accompanied by a young male, often leave to establish their own pride, very often on the fringes of their parent territory. In such circumstances, communication is not entirely severed, and much affectionate head-rubbing and face-licking accompany any chance meetings, although neither pride usually allows the other close access to its cubs.

Prior to reaching full maturity, young Lions of two and a half to three and a half years of age, not yet mature enough to challenge the leadership of the dominant males and possibly resenting their authority, usually leave the pride. Apart from attaining independence and therefore a firm base to develop into maturity, this consuetude also reduces the possibility of incestuous breeding. Within a short period, if not immediately, these young males normally pair up with a contemporary, very often a brother. Apart from facilitating more successful hunting tactics, the partnership provides a strong and enduring emotional bond in which much affection is usually apparent. There is rarely any tension or fighting in such a relationship, and the question as to who shall be the leader seems to resolve more around age than size.

The first priority of an independent sub-adult male pair is to establish a territory of their own. This they do by patrolling the perimeter, marking with urine, and by roaring. Humans can hear a roar from at least seven kilometres, and Lions with their more acute faculty, probably from a far greater distance. On several occasions when following Lions by vehicle at night, distant roars have instantly caused them visible alarm and resulted in a hasty retreat to well within their own territory. Should prides accidentally meet, previous encounters will often have established superiority and result in an immediate withdrawal by the subordinate group. In most instances, however, a give-away call or roar serves to alert and allow a tactful change of direction.

On reaching physical maturity, male pairs are in a position to challenge established rivals for pride leadership. If they are successful, the bond between them remains as firm as ever as they combine their talents to protect the pride from intruders, or other males, intent on relinquishing them of their dominant role. In fact, they often spend considerable time away from their acquired prides, probably preferring their own company in an acknowledgement of a more permanent relationship.

Tourists, accustomed to seeing Lions lying sleepily in the shade, can be pardoned for thinking them lazy, sloppy beasts. When prey almost stumbles upon them, their clumsy efforts to catch it often seem most inadequate. However, as night falls and the air temperature drops, they become progessively more agile. There is a definite correlation between air temperature and their agility. During the heat of the day, large males especially show difficulty in breathing, their bodies heaving with the effort. Even a short run at this time will leave them exhausted. Consequently, well over ninety percent of kills at Savuti are made at night and in the first hour of daylight.

Although most kills occur during the hours of darkness, there are obvious restrictions to nocturnal observation, chiefly concerning visibility by spotlight and unintentional influencing of the outcome by unavoidable interference. The prime time to study the hunting tactics of Lions is therefore at dawn. Unfortunately the frequency of kills at this time is rather limited. Ideally a combination of the two methods is necessary to achieve optimum results.

The essential tool for night-time observation is the radio collar (much disliked by photographers). Each collar has a tiny transmitter implanted in it, and each transmitter its own frequency. It is therefore possible by means of a directional finder to home in on any particular collared Lion at any time. Obviously it is not necessary to collar every Lion in a pride, but only a few carefully selected individuals. Collars are placed on these Lions once they have been immobilized by darting.

Typical procedure is to home in on the selected pride just before darkness, as it is easier to navigate difficult terrain or find them in thick bush during daylight. Once located, the Lions are likely to be lying lazily about as air temperatures at Savuti do not usually drop much during the first few hours of darkness. In order to be forewarned, should they decide to depart, a small spotlight can be trained on one of them. Once the Lions are on the move, two powerful hand-held spotlights are needed to follow the predators. One of these is used to find suitable routes around bushes and tall grass; the other to keep track of the Lions and also to pick up any prey's eyes. Since the spotlights are held from a position on top of the vehicle's roof to enable penetration over bush and tall grass, the observer is very often aware well in advance of the Lions of any nearby prey.

SAVUTI

Once prey is located, it is important to attempt not to influence the hunt's outcome. The various animals react to spotlights differently. Impala may be rendered immobile by blinding and care has to be taken not to shine lights directly at them. On the other hand, Zebra are likely to be frightened off, and it is necessary when coming across them to switch off both lights and engine and to rely on sounds for information as to the hunt's progress. Buffalo, when attacked, pay little attention to either, and it is possible to follow the Lions all the way in for the kill.

My introduction to night-time observation of Lions occurred when accompanying the Lion research team established at Savuti, who are doing useful studies in this field. The amazing aspect of the whole procedure is that, in areas where Lions are used to vehicles, they soon become accustomed to spotlights and being followed at night. No doubt the fact they are unable to escape detection because of their radio collars is conducive to an attitude of resignation and acceptance. In areas where they are less familiar with vehicles and are not collared, I have had limited success in following them in this manner.

An air of expectancy accompanies the setting of the sun in the African bush and animals prepare themselves for the vigils of the night ahead. As darkness falls an eerie silence envelopes the land, infinitely magnifying even the smallest of sounds. The cracking of a branch as an Elephant feeds some distance off shatters the silence like a gunshot. The unearthly howl of the Hyena, beginning with its low hoarse moan, and slowly rising through the octaves to end in a high-pitched scream, causes an involuntary shudder in the human sitting safely in the glow of his campfire. His imagination momentarily fantasises, placing him as an Impala that must be constantly alert if it is to see the light of dawn again. Alternatively, what would it be like to be a Lion stalking its prey in the blackness?

The hunt begins as one of the females walks off into the darkness. One by one the others rise and with much stretching and yawning, begin to follow. Heads down below the level of their shoulders, they walk one after another in a disciplined manner, but not necessarily in single file. Each Lion is in close contact with those immediately in front; thus, should the leaders stop, the rest will follow as one body. Suddenly, without any visible signals, they freeze. Each Lion strives to pick up sounds that will indicate the presence and position of prey. Then, the listening period over, they relax. For a few minutes there is some affectionate head-rubbing before they are off again. The direction is, whenever possible, into the wind so that they will be able to pick up any prey's scent and themselves remain undetected. Every ten minutes or so they stop to listen. Once more they freeze, and remain like this for only a few moments before splitting up and soundlessly melting into the night.

The bush is thick but the spotlight penetrates over it to pick up prey's eyes a kilometre away. A second quick sweep of the spotlight shows that the Lions are all quietly stalking in different directions. Two are proceeding to the right of the prey, the rest to the left. Each Lion moves without any hesitation, knowing exactly where it is going.

It is still half a kilometre to the prey. The Lions on the right are now well out of contact with those on the left. The prey, a magnificent Waterbuck bull, is grazing blissfully unaware of his hunters. By now the Lions have all disappeared into the darkness. Absolute stillness heightens the tension, the senses are alert with expectation. Suddenly, the Waterbuck lifts his head and stands listening. Some sixth sense warns him of danger. Then instinctively, with a desperate leap as he hears a rustle behind him, he sprints for his life, closely pursued by the two Lionesses which had gone off to the right.

The chase is on, the adversaries evenly matched for speed. It begins to look as though the Waterbuck's headstart may see him to safety. Then, like a flash, two more Lionesses streak from cover. They race to intercept the antelope who is not even aware of the fifth Lioness until she hits him at full speed, knocking him to the ground. In an instant, before the long horns can be used, a Lioness darts in and grips the throat. The Waterbuck defenceless, the pride begins to feed whilst the remaining Lioness continues to grip the throat in vicelike jaws until strangulation is complete.

The killing over, I become aware of my own tension as it physically and mentally dissipates. The last few action-packed minutes have been totally absorbing. Those sleepy daytime Lions have undergone a complete personality change. Their speed and power have become phenomenal, the method and organisation employed in the hunt optimally efficient. No wonder the Kalahari bushmen, those little wild men who understand animals better than anyone else, fear and respect Lions far more at night than during the day.

All the senses in Lions are particularly well developed. However, after watching several such hunts, one cannot but wonder just how well they can actually hear. Very often it is quite obvious that scent and sight have played no part in a particular prey detection. In the above instance, eyesight was rendered useless as there was a kilometre of thick bush between the Lions and their prey. Furthermore, it was a windless night as is often the case at Savuti, and there was little possibility of their catching the Waterbuck's scent from such a distance. Unbelievable as it may seem, taking into consideration the magnification of sound at night, it would appear that Lions can hear the ripping of grass as an animal grazes from at least a kilometre away.

Another remarkable aspect of most hunts is the manner in which Lions communicate and carry out complex attack strategies. Their immediate grasp of the situation and the automatic role assumption is all the more surprising considering the different attack plans used in various situations. Basically, roles can be divided into those of either catchers or chasers. Does each pride member have an allocated position in every situation? Probably this would be assuming too much. More likely, experience, training and finely-tuned instinct enable individuals to instantly fill a role and carry it out efficiently and in co-ordination with the rest of the pride.

Training for the hunt begins soon after birth. Cubs never tire of stalking one another, practising the various killing positions as they wrestle, or throwing their playmates to the ground in exactly the same manner as they will their future prey. When only a few months old, they are able to keep up with the adults on the nightly hunt. Their bearing glows with pride and self-importance, just as that of schoolboys who have qualified for a favourite outing. The entire excursion is enjoyed immensely and so they learn very quickly.

Two or three Lionesses will normally act as nursemaids throughout a hunt — one in front of the cubs, another behind them. Since the adults move at a steady pace, the cubs soon learn to walk in single-file as they concentrate on keeping up. Listening periods present a golden opportunity for a quick rough and tumble; however, their natural hunting instinct rapidly emerges and they also learn when not to risk the adults' displeasure.

Should the pride capture and not bother to kill a small animal such as a Buffalo calf, the Savuti Lions' favourite dish, one of the cubs may be allowed to lie across the struggling animal's neck to practise pinning it to the ground as the adults enjoy their meal. As the cubs grow larger, Lionesses sometimes permit them to pull down cornered or severely wounded and relatively harmless prey. First attempts are not often successful, since their techniques are far from polished. It may take them agonisingly long to dislodge the unfortunate animal from its feet. Eventually they are old enough to be incorporated into the attack plan, although probably always at first following an adult. Quite some time before becoming fully mature, they are capable killers and well able to fend for themselves. At this stage, as mentioned above, they may, depending on circumstances, leave the pride.

SAVUTI

The behaviour of Lions, as with most animal species, varies considerably in different parts of Africa. The Southern Kalahari Lion, for instance, has a very dissimilar lifestyle to his Savuti counterpart. Both have adapted to their respective types of terrain and prey, and have formulated their routines and hunting tactics accordingly. Even within the Chobe Park, the habits of prides vary immensely. One pride in the dry area often kills baby Elephants, but most Lions at Savuti would probably not even think of trying, although such kills have been recorded.

Essentially, Lions are individuals, and although one can generalize about their behaviour, it is impossible to lay down any hard and fast rules. A good example of this is Scarface, a member of one of the smaller and mainly sub-adult Savuti prides. Although extremely small, she is quite fearless and will attack adult Buffalo without hesitation; something the rest of the pride rarely do in her absence. On two occasions I have seen her jump on the rumps of mature Hippo as if to attempt to collapse their hindquarters. It seemed to me that because of their bulk there was little she could hope to achieve except possibly have some fun. However, who knows? Hippo with clawmarks on their rumps are not uncommon.

A popular misconception is that male Lions do no killing. Because of their immense size and strength, they automatically assume supremacy on the feeding register. Therefore, some lazy but possibly wise males make a habit of simply following the hunt and then appropriating their share, if not all of a smaller prey. Generally, however, most males play an active part in the hunt, their superior strength being invaluable in pulling down larger prey. Bachelor males, after all, do not have the advantage of a pride to help them hunt, and this serves to illustrate their efficiency as predators. It is certainly not uncommon to come across one of them with an Impala kill, a most difficult antelope to catch, although Buffalo are more their forte.

The first hour of daylight is the time the visitor to Savuti is likely to see a kill, and Buffalo the probable prey. Herds at the marsh rarely number less than several hundred, and when on the move, providing there is no dew, kick up large dustclouds which can be seen for several kilometres. On spotting such a dustcloud, it is worth taking a closer look as it may be Lions that are causing the Buffalo to stampede.

An adult Buffalo can be a dangerous and formidable foe. When combined in large numbers, their sanctity should be impenetrable. However, apart from a few of the dominant bulls, they lose all their individuality in a large herd, instinctively following those in front of them. Even a small group would be more than a match for the largest of Lion prides should they remain back to back and tightly packed together when attacked. Knowing this, the Savuti Lions have formulated relatively safe and yet simple methods of separating individuals from a herd.

Once the Buffalo have been spotted, the Lions advance at a trot making no attempt to conceal themselves. Instead of remaining close together, they purposefully string out intent on intensifying their presence, possibly even using the wind to carry their scents to the intended prey. Uneasily, the mass of black bodies pack tightly together and begin to mill around in the face of the approaching danger. They remain safely together in one impenetrable body until the Lions are only a few metres away, then one of the outsiders, insecure in his position, panics and attempts to bore into the greater safety of the mass. His action is relayed, and in a moment the herd is in a stampede, all blindly following those in front.

As the hunt proceeds, dust is everywhere and visibility only a few feet, so that it makes little difference whether it is night or day. At night, the atmosphere does seem somewhat more electrified as the spotlights struggle to penetrate the dust. The Lions are acting as individuals by now, attempting to divide the herd into smaller units. Every now and then, human heartbeats accelerate wildly as a black mass of stampeding bodies, hotly pursued by Lions, narrowly misses the Land Rover. Then, on some tacit signal, several massive Buffalo bulls detach themselves from the rest and shoulder to shoulder charge the Lions. So overpowering is the sight of these magnificent animals that all other activity momentarily fades into obscurity. The awesome power they generate as they charge aptly qualifies them for their nickname "The Heavies".

Fortunately, or unfortunately, they are too slow to cause the Lions any serious problems. Indeed, it is almost comical to watch the ease with which the predators avoid their rushes, almost to the point of ignoring them, whilst concentrating on the main body in the hope of singling out a calf. If the herd is very large, as is often the case, dust will rise many metres into the air enveloping the entire scene. All one can then do is sit and wait for the high-pitched bleat which signifies that a calf has been caught, or the lower moan of an adult. It is amazing that with all the noise made by thousands of stampeding hooves, the bleat is easily heard and succeeds for a moment in stopping time in the realisation of death.

Frequently, two or even three calves may be killed in a hunt. Occasionally an adult, usually a female, may also be taken in this manner. Buffalo are often in the presence of death, and as soon as a calf or comrade is down, it ceases to exist for the rest of the herd. Sometimes, in the confusion of several thousand Buffalo stampeding in different directions all in a small area, prey may be at least temporarily released from death as the predators are forced to dodge the oncoming stampede. If such a Buffalo is badly mutilated and large enough to be dangerous, the Lions will wait for it to weaken considerably from loss of blood before moving in to finish it off (Plate 218). Having to kill night after night, their tactics are at all times highly logical and risks are cut to a minimum.

Animal life and death is cruel by our emotional human standards, prey often being eaten when it is still alive. This is not a result of thoughtlessness by the predators, but rather of logical necessity. For instance, if Lions are hungry and the pride large, none of them may wish to sacrifice the limited eating time available to throttle a harmless Buffalo calf. Alternatively, an adult Buffalo with its huge bulk of up to a ton and its massive boss, is an exceedingly dangerous prey. Consequently, once its hindquarters have been collapsed, it is likely to be eaten alive from the back since the Lions will wish to avoid injury by staying well out of reach of the horns.

Buffalo calves form the staple diet of the Chobe's Lions. They are plentiful, and to catch them is relatively easy and risk-free. However, an adult Buffalo is a feast for all, and although the success to attempted kills ratio is not very high, the predators have evolved a surprisingly low-risk method of hunting them.

The majority of adult Buffalo preyed upon by the Savuti Lions are either solitary bulls or members of small bachelor groups usually past their prime. A Buffalo in the security of thick bush will aggressively turn on any attackers. On the other hand, if in open territory, even the largest of bulls will rarely change their minds and attempt to defend themselves once put to flight. Therefore, on sighting such a prey, Lions will attempt to panic it into an isolated and single-minded dash for cover. With supreme effortlessness, almost as if in slow motion, they then close the gap and in an action reminiscent of schoolboys playing leapfrog, line up and spring on the fleeing animal's rump in an effort to collapse its hindquarters. A male Lion may weigh in excess of two hundred and twenty kilogrammes, and a Buffalo's immense power is amply evident as it momentarily supports each clinging predator, hardly altering the tempo of its stride. Once a Buffalo reaches cover, it will back its hindquarters safely into a bush so that only its front is vulnerable – far too risky a proposition for any predator.

SAVUTI

Lions do frequently succeed in collapsing adult Buffaloes' hindquarters. There can be no meaningful success to attempted kills ratio, as this will depend entirely on the capabilities of the individual Lion or pride concerned. Once the predators have the unfortunate animal pinned to the ground, they eat it from the back keeping well clear of the horns. Testicles are often bitten off to ensure the Buffalo bleeds to death more quickly. No matter how natural, the violence and pain involved as the animal pathetically moans in agony as it is eaten alive, is usually too excessive for the newcomer to the scene. On occasions where one of the attackers is offered the opportunity to dart in and grip the throat, perhaps for a split second after a particularly bad fall, suffocation may take many minutes. Much will depend on the strength of the individual Lion's jaws, ten minutes probably being about an average.

It is usually a sign that Lions are about to hunt when several pride members start to hone their claws on a tree in much the same manner as a domestic cat. Apart from gripping onto a fleeing Buffalo's back and so lacerating the skin, Lions may also attempt to sever the spinal column with a bite. Since the success to attempted kills ratio is not that high, there are always Savuti Buffalo wandering about with mutilated hindquarters. Pecking oxpeckers, the merciless sun, perpetual dust, and flies all hinder the healing process. In order to avoid all this, these Buffalo often spend their days lying with their wounds underwater (especially in the relatively predator-free section of the channel by the campsite), until a protective scab has formed. Fish, mainly barbel, may nibble irritatingly at the wound causing them to lie with their rumps pressed against the bank. Unfortunately, the wounds often turn septic, resulting in a slow and painful death.

Savuti plays host to numerous Hyena clans, and the continual interaction between them and Lions is highly relevant to any study of the latter. As yet, no nocturnal studies using radio collars have been undertaken into their ways in this area. Unfortunately, their eyesight seems less adaptable to spotlights than that of Lions, making this task doubly difficult.

In the early mornings, familiar groups or solitary Hyenas can be seen returning along habitual paths from the night's activities. They enjoy spending the first part of the day chewing a selected bone, and generally watching the world go by whilst lying in a shallow depression so that only their heads are visible above ground level. As the sun becomes hotter, they usually depart for the coolness of an underground burrow, although prone to lying for long periods submerged in a marsh pool with only their noses protruding above the surface.

Unlike most predators, the female is slightly larger than the male, and therefore dominant. Their clan-structure seems to be far looser than that of Lion prides, and they join together in large numbers to hunt, defend their territory, or scavenge food. Females suckle only their own, the young being entirely dependent on mother's milk and not joining adults at kills until well into their first year.

Commonly, territorial behaviour occurs between members of the same species. For instance, Lions will jealously chase members of other prides off their territory, but not Hyenas or Jackals. However, on several occasions I have witnessed Hyenas in pursuit of small sub-adult prides, apparently seeing them off the territory. This does not seem unreasonable behaviour since both species depend to a large extent on the same prey. Particularly interesting is the fact that the Hyenas in most instances hardly outnumbered the Lions. Perhaps they were given the task by more numerous clan members who had initially put the Lions to flight.

It would be very interesting to establish the respective percentages of food the Chobe Hyenas obtain from hunting, scavenging, and the expropriation of kills. Since their lives are so interwoven night after night, Hyenas are intimately familiar with the personalities of the various

Lions in their common territory. Should they come across a strange pride at a kill, they will often attempt to expropriate the carcass for themselves. Summoned by the weird and yet meaningful vocabulary of their kind (a series of indescribable howls, moans and insane sounding laughter), they will slowly gather forces a short distance from the kill. Eventually, when psyched up enough and in sufficient numbers, they slowly advance on the feeding Lions. They do this in a rough semi-circle, tails high in an aggressive posture, and all the time making an enormous unearthly din (Plate 161). If the Lions are not susceptible to their bluff, the Hyenas will halt at the last possible moment, possibly two metres distant. Should one of them unwisely overstep the safety limit, the least it can hope for is a severe mauling. There is no love lost between the two species.

Once Hyenas have tested Lions in this way, they will not normally attempt to forcibly expropriate a kill again if unsuccessful in the first instance. Large prides are Hyena-proof; however, should only a few members be present, the situation may alter. Essentially, it is the presence of particular individuals that makes the difference; Hyenas soon learn which Lions can be intimidated and which cannot. The attendance of a mature male is usually decisive. I have seen one solitary and bloated Lion lying peacefully and protectively next to his kill, completely ignoring a large accumulation of twenty or thirty clamouring Hyenas. No doubt they had to wait for his lordship to depart in his own time before obtaining anything to eat.

It is interesting to note that in October of 1979, a mob of over sixty hyenas was seen ganging up on Savuti Lions at a kill. Predator activity and competition for prey was, however, exceptionally intense during that period due to the earlier than normal dissipation of waterholes in the corridor.

In early days, it was commonly supposed that Hyenas existed entirely by scavenging, that they were cowardly, and even hermaphroditic. Today we know that although scavengers (as are most predators), they are also capable hunters, and the sexes are distinguishable. Their incredibly powerful jaws are not only capable of chewing into digestible form bones too tough for other predators, but also well-suited to hunting.

Generally, they group together in packs to hunt, but they do also make their own kills. On one occasion, I came across a Hyena, belly bulging almost to capacity, standing over a partially eaten Impala (Plate 164). At first glance it occurred to me that the antelope had died from some illness, or that the Hyena had expropriated the kill from a Cheetah. However, an examination of the tracks showed that a considerable struggle had taken place with the Hyena the killer. Surprisingly, he was left alone to eat his meal in peace — with their acute sense of smell Hyenas rarely remain ignorant of a fresh kill for long.

Exciting as the Buffalo/Lion interaction at Savuti may be, Buffalo are relatively easy prey. A large herd is by no means inconspicuous, and the predators have the advantage of superior speed. On the other hand, Tsessebe and Impala can easily outrun Lions, and are the ultimate test to their abilities as hunters. The Tsessebe is the fastest of African antelope, the Impala a mercurial dodger and jumper.

It is indeed a comical sight to see an Impala mischievously taunting the king of beasts for the fun of it; a favourite although infrequent pastime when a ram comes across a solitary Lion lying half-asleep during the daytime. The predator is intent only on spending the blistering midday hours as lazily and peacefully as possible; however, there is no accounting for instinct. Cheekily, with much prancing and snorting, the performing ram parades tantalisingly close to the sleepy predator, who at first tries his best to ignore the insolent upstart. Nevertheless, peace and sleep are impossible, and the blissful midday tranquillity completely destroyed. The ram then challengingly steps just that much closer to the agitated predator, who can no longer resist attempting to catch

SAVUTI

it. Effortlessly, almost insultingly, the dodging antelope easily evades the Lion. Hardly has the heavily-panting predator returned to the shelter of his bush when the irritating antelope is back again and in top form. Another futile chase follows, the Impala prancing around, almost taking a bow and thoroughly enjoying himself. And so the performance continues, eventually leaving one bad tempered and thoroughly annoyed Lion, definitely the loser in the encounter.

Impala are both browsers and grazers. They rarely spend time in the open, preferring the Acacia bush and woodland surrounding the grassy plains and alongside the channel. Consequently, there is usually cover available for any stalking predator.

The attack plan is simple, yet very difficult to execute. On locating the feeding antelope, the Lions immediately split up, each silently melting into the surroundings. Such is their stealth that even if close by, they usually all soon disappear from the observer's view. Impala have keen senses, their sight, smell and hearing all being more than adequate. Should one of them become aware of a movement at this stage, the hunt will have to be abandoned. The Lions concentrate on taking up positions on three sides of the feeding antelope, the fourth being left open as a result of the give-away wind. Bit by bit the net then closes until the stalking predators are only a few metres distant. A high-pitched snort sounds the alarm, and instantaneously the confused antelope leap in all directions in ignorance of their attackers' positions or numbers. Then, as one, the Lions emerge from cover in a frantic dash to single out and encircle one of the fleeing antelope. For a moment the activity isolates a world of airborne Impala and racing Lions. The attention is abruptly riveted on one unfortunate animal frantically endeavouring to dodge several Lions who are almost on him. One jump in the wrong direction and it is all over.

In the early mornings the wiry coppercoated Tsessebe can often be seen bounding about the marsh in high spirits. With legs that appear to be spring-loaded, and knees that hardly bend when they run, the effect is as if they are bouncing along on pogosticks. However effortless this looks, the speed of the animal is quite phenomenal. It is also a good dodger, highly alert, and usually found in groups. During the day they can be seen in large numbers grazing on the southern section of the marsh, often alongside Zebra and Wildebeest.

At dusk the Tsessebe herds usually separate from slower and less gifted companions, but nevertheless normally remain on the open plains. Since there is very little cover available in such habitat, it is almost impossible for Lions to stalk up close to them undetected. The previous strategy often used for Impala is therefore of little use.

Lions are superbly camouflaged, their tan-coloured coats blending perfectly with the dry grass of the Savuti plains. Most animals, no matter how sharp their eyesight, are mainly receptive to movement, not recognising stationary form unless very close. A keen-sighted Tsessebe will detect the slightest movement from a great distance off. Therefore, optimal use of a Lion's camouflaged coat occurs when the predator is stationary.

Lions regularly mount the numerous termite hills on the plains in order to obtain long and unobstructed views of the surrounding territory. Consequently, the Tsessebe herd will probably be some considerable distance off when spotted. The catchers are the first to take their positions, downwind from the antelope, and in the probable flightpath. They string themselves out in a relatively evenly-spaced interception line, making use of any available cover no matter how insignificant. Once in position, they settle down for a long and motionless wait.

In the meantime the chasers have made a large detour to approach undetected from the opposite side. Their biggest problem is the wind which must be carefully navigated if it is not to give their presence away. If possible, they will advance in a rough semi-circle so as to be in a position to influence the direction of the antelopes' flight. With the limited cover available, the chances of a successful stalk culminating in a kill are virtually nil. The predators must, however, remain undetected until they are in a close enough position to fulfil their role. When some thirty metres distant, one of the wary antelope spots them.

The chase is on, the swift-footed Tsessebe confidently fleeing, not even extended to full speed. The pursuers divide and race to the sides, initially steering the galloping antelope into the intended direction. Each catcher tenses in anticipation as the blissfully unaware prey fast approaches. Most of the Tsessebe flash past the waiting predators, but one is unlucky. Too late to dodge, the antelope virtually collides with the springing Lion. Such is its speed that the two tumble for some metres before coming to a halt in a tangle of finality.

If Lions have a favourite attack plan it is probably this one, since it lends itself to numerous applications. Given the capabilities of these largest of African predators, it is doubtful if the human mind could invent any more effective hunting methods. It is certainly unlikely that we could carry them out so efficiently, with such discipline, and accept failure with such dignity and farsightedness.

The night-time is the life time in the African bush. It is the time the barrel-shaped Hippo leaves the rivers to graze. Elephants, free from inhibitions, romp around waterholes like children playing games in the moonlight. Buffalo regain their self-confidence, and predators and their prey enact the timeless struggle for survival. Unfortunately, it is also the time that we humans, even with our spotlights and other sophisticated equipment, are unlikely ever to penetrate in any great depth. Thus, in spite of all our learning, the fascination for the African bush will remain, as it does for any unravelled mystery.

105

107

106

104 In 1957, after having been dry for a century, the Savuti Channel flowed once more, entering the Mababe Depression (once a huge lake) through the Makwikwe Sandridge to terminate shortly thereafter in the marshy plain visible ahead.

105 After travelling through the flat featureless terrain of the Mababe Depression, several rocky outcrops no more than a few hundred feet in height herald the approach to Savuti.

106 Lions have remarkably fine eyesight. From the elevated positions offered by the rocky outcrops, they can survey the surrounding territory for many kilometres in search of prey.

107 A large herd of several thousand Buffalo graze on the marsh in the late afternoon. Buffalo especially calves, are the staple diet of the Savuti Lions.

108

109

110

108 Having decided to attack a Buffalo herd, Lions will usually advance at a trot making no attempt to conceal themselves. Their aim is to panic the ungulates into a blind stampede with the object of separating a calf from the main body.

109 As the hunt proceeds, several large bulls, often referred to as 'the heavies', detach themselves from the milling mass and charge the lions. Fortunately, or unfortunately, they are too slow to cause any serious problems and the predators easily avoid their rushes with the minimum of effort.

110 Buffalo are often in the presence of death, and once a calf is down it ceases to exist for the rest of the herd who leave the area as fast as possible.

111 Even though bloated to capacity (they can eat almost a quarter of their body weight in one sitting), Lions often linger for hours beside a kill to chew those specially tasty bits.

112 Solitary Buffalo bulls can be extremely dangerous animals since their natural inclination on feeling threatened may be to attack. Should they decide one's approach is close enough, they will normally lower and then shake their heads warningly. Surprisingly, when in large herds they become almost timid with the loss of their individuality.

111

112

113

113 Hippo and Elephant enjoy a typical section of the channel.

114 Several ungulates, particularly Impala and Giraffe, frequently eat the fine sand of termite mounds (termitaria) as it is particularly rich in mineral content brought up from the subsoil by the termites.

116

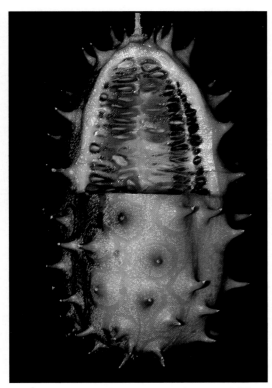

117

115 Botswana's Lions are noted for their size. Here, a massive Savuti male weighing about 200 kg sports a splendid Metro Goldwyn Mayer mane. Lionesses weigh considerably less, averaging 120 to 130 kg, but weights of up to 180 kg have been recorded.

116 In an effort to relieve her indigestion after a large meal, a Lioness rocks backwards and forwards on a sloping branch.

117 A colourful and edible wild melon *(Cucumis metuliterus)*.

118 On or shortly after leaving their parent pride, young male Lions often pair up with a contemporary, sometimes a brother. Apart from facilitating more successful hunting tactics, the partnership provides a strong and enduring emotional bond in which much affection is usually apparent.

118

120

119 To reach down to drink, Giraffe must spread their legs apart in a particularly awkward fashion which renders them virtually helpless if attacked by Lions. Consequently, they usually spend long periods searching every bit of surrounding cover before submitting themselves to this vulnerable position.

120 Common behaviour; a Whitebacked Vulture does the goosestep in an effort to impress his colleagues with his ferocity in the hope of securing a good position at the carcass.

121 Much squabbling and pecking at each other usually accompanies the consumption of a carcass by vultures. Afterwards, the ground may be carpeted with feathers for metres around.

121

122 Unable to resist the temptation, several members of a pride sheltering in the midday shade of a dead plains tree, prepare to attack a herd of Zebra. Notice the large male amongst those taking the initiative.

123 Although another or other pride members may have actually made the kill, dominant male Lions often claim small prey, such as this Tsessebe fawn, for themselves.

124 Sporting impressive spiralling horns a Kudu bull comments to his companion on the irritating antics of the photographer. Essentially browsers, they are mainly nocturnal feeders and spend much of the day resting concealed in the shade.

125 Dead trees, with branches trailing like ghostly arms, make a last stand against the flowing river.

122

124

123

126

126 Elephant bulls frequently wander through the campsite and will often browse within a few metres of humans or gingerly step over a guyrope to reach a tasty morsel in an overhanging tree. They seem to recognise that this is man's territory and normally accept his sovereignty in the area.

127 On becoming aware of the photographer, a Crocodile instinctively bolts for the water. Although extremly shy, they are plentiful in the Savuti Channel. Their main diet consists of fish, especially the prolific barbel, supplemented by the occasional bird, small mammal, or antelope.

128 When collecting firewood, it is not uncommon to come across bats sleeping in hollowed out tree stumps.

127

128

129

130

131

129 Large concentrations of gregarious Tsessebe, the swiftest of all African antelope, usually frequent the central and southern sections of the marshy plains.

130 & 131 The result of a herd's unwise decision to cross the corridor in the dry season. A dehydrated calf struggles to regain his feet before extending a tiny trunk to touch the Land Rover in a desperate plea for help. After a heated discussion, we decided not to give him water as his frantic mother nearby might then have left him. Solitary calves of this size quickly fall prey to Lion prides.

132 A herd of Elephants migrate northwards across the dry corridor towards the lifegiving Chobe River.

135

136

133 A blur of action and gaping mouths prevail as two Hippo bulls fight over the territorial right to a section of the channel.

134 With surprising speed and leaving a wake comparable to that of a powerboat, the victor chases the vanquished off his territory. Although only adequate swimmers, Hippo possess a specific gravity higher than that of water enabling them to move across the bottom remarkably fast.

135 Perched on a favourite branch, a Pied Kingfisher studies the river for signs of small fish. On sighting one, he will hover several metres above the surface, then, with startling speed dive on the unsuspecting victim to catch it in his beak. Before consuming the struggling fish, the bird will normally beat it lifeless on a branch.

136 Hippo often remain undetected in surprisingly small pools by pushing their nostrils gently up through floating weed or vegetation when they need to breath.

137

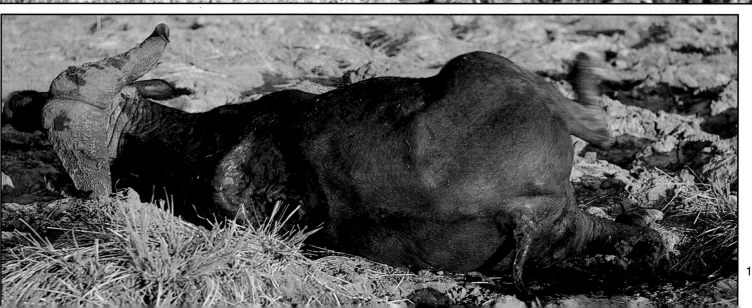

138

137 Highly inquisitive, Buffalo will often stare fascinated at nearby humans.

138 An adult Buffalo bull, with one leg broken, his spine severed, and a huge chunk of his shoulder eaten, vainly struggles to regain his feet. His prey defenceless, a huge male Lion simply ate his fill and left.

139

140–142

139 Living in a remote region of the park and not being sure of our human status, this snarling pride protectively surrounds a newly killed Buffalo calf, thinking that we may attempt to expropriate it.

140–142 A Buffalo calf, such as this one, provides insufficient food and feeding space for a large pride. Much growling and position jockeying will occur between those members large enough to qualify for a place at the carcass; the others go hungry.

143

144

143 Much sought after as trophies by hunters, the Roan Antelope has disappeared from most of Africa. Only their extreme alertness and cunning have enabled them to survive in remote areas.

144 In many parts of Africa the gregarious Zebra provide Lions with a good proportion of their meals. However, at Savuti they lead a much less hazardous existence due to the profusion of far easier to catch Buffalo.

145 The Crowned Plover lays its eggs in a scrape in the ground. It will rush about intruders who are near the scrape, screeching its noisy and irritating 'kie-wieets' until they leave the vicinity.

145

146 Despised by most, the Whitebacked Vulture is rarely given credit for its attractive plumage or essential role in nature.

147 A pack of African Wild Dogs gather in the shade. They are highly gregarious, mainly diurnal, and probably provide an even better example of harmonious interdependence than Lion prides. Males and females share most tasks such a hunting, feeding and protecting the puppies.

146

148

148 A large pack of African Wild Dogs may average several kills per day. They have the highest success ratio of attacks to kills of the larger predators and once they have pulled down prey they literally disembowel and eat it in minutes, bolting down the meat in chunks.

149 African Wild Dog pups lie pressed against each other in a circle of togetherness. Litter size may be up to a dozen or more, the cubs being raised in a den (usually an old Hyena warren) for the first two or three months of their lives. They are fully weaned at about five to six weeks, but they do eat regurgitated meat received from adults well before this.

150 Silhouetted against a vibrant Savuti sunset, a herd of Giraffe tower above the distant horizon. Nearly 6 metres in height, they are the tallest animals on earth.

149

147

151 A proud and exaggerated yawn. Large animals that use their teeth as weapons, particularly Lions and Hippos, will often put on such displays to discourage a closer approach by intruders.

152 Spotted Hyenas in typical posture over the remains of a Buffalo kill. Unlike most predators, the female is slightly larger than the male and therefore dominant. Their clan structure is far looser than that of Lion prides but they do join together in large numbers to facilitate such activities as hunting, scavenging or defending their territories.

153 Heuglin's Robin, a frequent visitor to campsites along the Chobe, is regarded by many as having the most beautiful calls of any bird.

154

156

155

154 Shortly after giving birth, a Hippo cow lies exhausted on the bank a two year old calf beside her. Even oxpeckers, pecking painfully at her tender umbilical chord cannot stir her into movement.

155 On becoming aware of humans in the vicinity, a second cow temporarily assumes the role of foster mother and nudges the newly-born calf in an effort to make it stand.

156 Once it is firmly on its feet, she guides it to the water and safety.

157 The Elephant has twenty-four molars (chewing teeth), six on either side of the upper and lower jaws. When molar number one becomes worn, it moves forward and drops out, and is replaced by number two. Molar number six is the final one to come into wear, and as it wears down the Elephant is able to chew less and less food into digestible form and eventually starves. Such is the sad position of this old lady who can no longer keep up with the herd. Note the hollow temples, the pronounced ribs, and the excrement on her hindquarters.

157

158

160

158 Since the ratio of successful Lion attacks on adult Savuti Buffalo is not very high, there are always quite a few of these ungulates wandering about with badly mutilated hindquarters. In this instance, pecking oxpeckers open up recently healed scabs from such a wound. Notice the bitten off tail – not uncommon.

159 Adult Lions are noted for their inactivity during the daytime; cubs are forever on the go. Therefore, if the pride is large and there are several litters, cubs will often be deposited under bushes or other cover a short distance away where they can play to their heart's content. Here, a Lioness whose misfortune it is to act as nursemaid for the day, keeps a wary eye open for intruders.

160 An avid scavenger, the Yellowbilled Kite often frequents campsites, daringly pouncing on unguarded food. Particularly adept at gliding, their tail feathers are formed to make an ideal rudder.

161 Tails up in an aggressive posture, in a rough semi-circle, and making an enormous unearthly din, Hyenas advance on a Lioness.

162 Clearly not susceptible to their bluff she ignores them until they overstep the limit. Then, like a flash, she angrily turns and lunges. If she had caught one of them, the least it could have hoped for was a severe mauling as there is no love lost between the two species.

163 Feeding priority in large prides depends mainly on the size of the individual. Small Lionesses, such as this one, rarely obtain their fair share of kills if prey is small or scarce; consequently, they are often in poor physical condition and prone to unnatural aggressive displays.

164 Hyenas generally hunt in packs, but they do also make solitary kills. On coming across this one standing over an Impala, it occured to me that the antelope may have died from sickness, or that the Hyena had expropriated it from a Cheetah. However, an examination of the tracks indicated that a considerable struggle had taken place with the Hyena the killer.

165 Enjoying an early morning drink at a crystal-clear marsh pool, Lionesses and their cubs unintentionally display the superbly conditioned muscles which leave them unchallenged as the most powerful of African predators.

164

166 The African Wild Dog, sporting the sleek and athletic lines of stamina and speed, can keep up this fast lope for many kilometres. They hunt in packs, usually chasing their prey until it falters from exhaustion and they can catch it.

167 A nursery of Impala fawns.

168 Irrespective of how much meat is left on a carcass, Hyenas will rarely allow a Jackal to feed alongside them. The smaller predator can often be seen hovering a few feet from the kill, waiting for an opportunity to dart in and snatch a piece of momentarily unguarded meat.

168

167

169

170

169 Lions normally temporarily leave the pride to mate, copulation occuring approximately every half hour (intervals can vary immensely) for many hours on end. The period immediately prior to each union is regularly accompanied by fierce snarling and face-pulling as the male attempts to impress and intimidate his conquest.

170 Once mounted, a lion may grip the top of the female's neck in his mouth to ensure co-operation throughout the act. The majority of Lionesses clearly show facial evidence of deep sensual pleasure during intercourse.

171

171 Lions are essentially individuals. This Lioness had an intense dislike of vehicles and would often mock charge the Land Rover if approached too close.

172 Leaving us in no doubt that she resents our intrusion, a Lioness interrupts her meal to growl threateningly in our direction.

173 The lashing of the tail in a quick jerky motion from side to side is a sure sign that a Lion or Lioness is becoming angry. The final indication before a charge is usually the pulling of the corners of the mouth backwards, as this Lioness is beginning to do.

174 December rainclouds hover menacingly over the Savuti Channel.

175 – 178 Although cow herds are relatively scarce at Savuti, the area has long been a favourite haunt of Elephant bulls. Very predictable in their habits, midday is the usual time for a drink and a swim in their favourite wet-season pool. They may spend hours cavorting around with each other, chasing any nearby Hippos, or simply rejoicing in the coolness of the refreshing water.

179

179 The migratory butterfly (*Belenois aurota*) feeding on energy giving nectar.

180 Saddlebilled Storks dancing during the mating season.

181 A magnificent Waterbuck bull. Although they usually live close to water, often taking refuge in reed beds, Waterbuck are by no means truly aquatic (unlike the Sitatunga) and may be found considerable distances from rivers or marshes.

180

182 There is definitely a correlation between air temperature and Lions' agility. Most of the day is usually spent sleeping or lying sloppily about, the nights being a time of action.

183 Although never venturing very high, most cubs love to climb trees where they tussle with playmates or simply enjoy an elevated status.

184 Just another of nature's
remarkable ways; from their first
steps onwards Impala young can
run almost as fast as their swift-
footed elders.

186 The tiny Barred Owl is
a frequent visitor to campsites
at night. It usually perches on a
branch often visible within the
circle of firelight, and every now
and then swoops to catch insects
attracted to the bright lantern
lights. Unlike most owls, it is also
relatively active during the
daytime.

189

190

187 Once old enough to follow the hunt, cubs soon learn to walk in single-file as they concentrate on keeping up.

188 Cubs contentedly suckle at a Lioness. Although they start to eat meat after developing canines at about four weeks old, suckling may continue for as long as six months or more.

189 & 190 Tired of trying to eat a tough Giraffe, cubs turn their efforts to more important things.

188

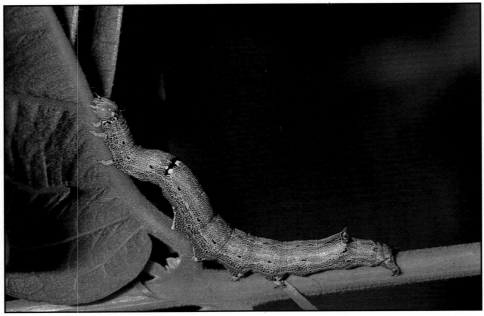

191 The first heavy rains usually herald the hatching of a multitude of finely patterned caterpillars.

192 Yellowbilled Storks pose against a background of February greenness.

193 An Impala bull stands stock still, eyes riveted on a spot. If other bulls in the vicinity are behaving similarly, it often pays to search the area they are looking at for predators.

191

192

196

194

194 A Waterbuck kill. It is often incorrectly thought that Lions do not prey on Waterbuck since the antelope's coat is impregnated with a foul tasting oily secretion supplied by the glands under the skin.

195 A dangerous position for these cubs. Fast becoming intolerant of them at a kill, one swipe of this adult male's paw could break a cub's back.

196 & 197 With the coming of the rains, endless swarms of insects bombard the campfire light. Attracted by this easy prey, frogs, rodents, scorpions and other small predators scuttle about in a frantic endeavour to secure their fill.

197

195

198 Graceful Impala pose, their glossy coats aglow
against a background of delicate wet-season colours.

199 Similar in physique to the fawn-coloured Roan, the majestic Sable is noted for its aggressiveness and may defend itself vigorously against Lions which rarely attack this antelope.

200 Buffalo frequently break off parts of their horns, sometimes in clashes with other bulls, more often as they sharpen the tips by goring the ground. Such buffalo are often bad tempered and should be left well alone.

201 Trunk extended to catch any scent, a cow inquisitively advances towards the photographer. Elephants have a superb sense of smell, more than adequate hearing, but relatively poor eyesight. Even if only a few paces away, it very often seems to be smell, not sight, that relays the final confirmation of identification to their brain.

202

203 – 207

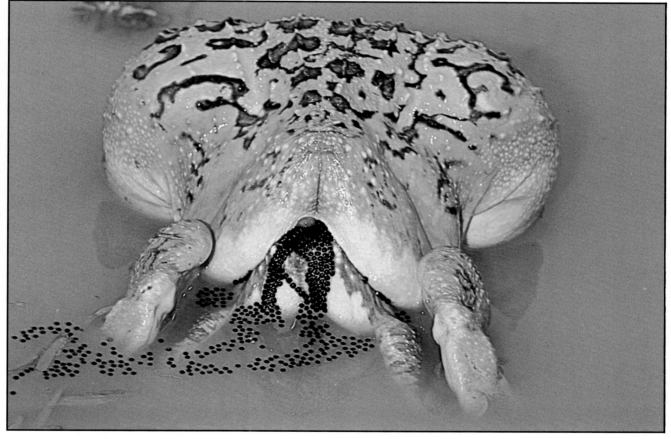

202 In the early mornings Impala can often be seen rejoicing in their agility. Although of only average speed for an antelope, they can effortlessly leap nine or ten metres in length and over three in height. Their mercurial dodging is a highly effective defense against attacking predators.

203 – 207 On approaching a large pool formed by December rains, we were surprised to see the surface alive with splashes. Closer investigation revealed numerous attractively coloured male Bullfrogs (*Pyxicephalus adspersus*) ferociously fighting each other over the rights to far less numerous females. All the contestants had broken skin around the head caused by opponents' bites, and blood was evident on the majority of individuals.
In most groups one Bullfrog would clearly end up dominant and cover the same female time and time again. No entry is effected, the male spraying his sperm to fertilize the female's eggs as they emerge. The next day not a single Bullfrog could be found.

208 A freshly excavated Warthog burrow beneath a termite mound. Mainly diurnal, warthogs usually sleep and breed in such burrows which they enter backwards so as to emerge tusks first. Not highly intelligent, they are sometimes panicked into rashly leaving their burrows as Lions calculatingly scratch the surface above the main chamber.

209 A Warthog sow tends her litter.

210 Locals keep well away from Hippos when paddling their mekoros (dugout canoes). These huge herbivores probably account for more human deaths than any other large African animal.

211 A colourful butterfly (*Charaxes jasius saturnus*) feeds on sap exuding from a plant recently stepped upon by some large animal. The female usually lays her eggs on the leaves of a bush or tree belonging to the Leguminosae. The egg hatches in seven days and the resultant green caterpillar moults four times over six weeks before fully maturing. The adult butterfly emerges after about three weeks of pupation.

211

212

214

212 Although this was her kill, because of her small size, a Lioness has difficulty in obtaining a place at the carcass.

213 Once pulled down, this Buffalo cow somehow managed to entangle her horns firmly in a dead tree. Taking advantage of the opportunity, a Lioness immediately seized the animal's throat and commenced strangulation. Notice the Lioness opening up the soft spot below the tail, and the Lion on top the junction of the right front leg and the body.

213

214 Puffadders account for the majority of snakebites in Africa as they have a habit of lying in paths, especially alongside rivers, and are often too lazy to move until stepped upon.

215 The nocturnal Porcupine, when threatened, will stick its vulnerable head into thick cover and turn a quill-covered back on the attacker. Alternatively, if there is no cover about, it may charge backwards. Quills can cause fatal wounds to predators and are dislodged from the Porcupine's body once the tips are buried in the attacker. They cannot shoot their quills as is often believed.

215

216

219

217

218

216 Sometimes, in the confusion of several thousand Buffalo stampeding in different directions all in a small area, prey may be at least temporarily released from death as Lions are forced to dodge the oncoming mass. If such is the case, the Buffalo may be badly mutilated, often with entrails hanging out.

217 & 218 If the mutilated Buffalo is large enough to be dangerous, the Lions will wait for it to weaken considerably from loss of blood before moving in to

finish it off. Having to kill night after night, their tactics are at all times highly logical and risks are cut to a minimum.

219 In a large pride, two or three Lionesses will normally act as nursemaids throughout the hunt.

220 Elephants drink at a favourite wet-season pan close to the Savuti campsite.

221–222

221 & 222 On guard! Two Tsessebe confront each other in a vigorous display of mock fighting. Seemingly possessed of endless energy, they can often be seen bounding about the marsh in the early mornings. With legs that appear to be spring loaded, and knees that hardly bend when they run, the effect is as if they are bouncing along on pogosticks.

223 A line of Giraffe cross a large Savuti pan. Denuded of vegetation for most of the year, magically, almost overnight, such pans become carpeted in succulent short green grass during the rainy season.

224 Hyenas are particularly fond of water and often spend the early mornings lying about in shallow pools. As the sun becomes hotter, they usually depart for the coolness of some underground burrow, although prone to lying for long periods submerged in a marsh pool with only their noses protruding above the surface.

225 A red African sun sets over the Savuti Channel as a herd of Buffalo come down through the dust for their evening drink and two Elephants wander contentedly off into the distance.